T0247908

GRADUAL

GRADUAL

THE CASE FOR INCREMENTAL
CHANGE IN A RADICAL AGE

GREG BERMAN

AND

AUBREY FOX

OXFORD
UNIVERSITY PRESS

OXFORD
UNIVERSITY PRESS

Oxford University Press is a department of the University of Oxford. It furthers
the University's objective of excellence in research, scholarship, and education
by publishing worldwide. Oxford is a registered trade mark of Oxford University
Press in the UK and certain other countries.

Published in the United States of America by Oxford University Press
198 Madison Avenue, New York, NY 10016, United States of America.

© Oxford University Press 2023

Library of Congress Cataloging-in-Publication Data
Names: Berman, Greg, author. | Fox, Aubrey, author
Title: Gradual : the case for incremental change in a radical age /
Greg Berman and Aubrey Fox.
Description: New York : Oxford University Press, 2023. |
Includes bibliographical references and index.
Identifiers: LCCN 2022035031 (print) | LCCN 2022035032 (ebook) |
ISBN 9780197637043 (hardback) | ISBN 9780197637067 (epub)
Subjects: LCSH: Political planning—United States. |
Public administration—United States—Decision making. |
Government accountability—United States. | Policy sciences—United States. |
Political culture—United States.
Classification: LCC JK468 .P64 B47 2023 (print) | LCC JK468 .P64 (ebook) |
DDC 320.60973—dc23/eng/20220923
LC record available at https://lccn.loc.gov/2022035031
LC ebook record available at https://lccn.loc.gov/2022035032

DOI: 10.1093/oso/9780197637043.001.0001

Printed by Sheridan Books, Inc., United States of America

What then are the "problems poorly stated" of our time? They are various but have, it seems to me, a unifying characteristic; namely, the rejection by those seeking a more just, more equal society of any indications that our society is in fact becoming more just and more equal. Society is seen in ahistorical terms: what is not altogether acceptable is altogether unacceptable; gradations are ignored and incremental movements scorned. Those who by disposition are incrementalists, or for whom the contemplation of society has led to a conviction that incremental change is a necessity, not a choice, in human affairs, are baffled by this attitude and resentful of it.

—Daniel Patrick Moynihan

Contents

Introduction

An Era of Radical Change?

In October 1787, Alexander Hamilton began work on *The Federalist Papers*, a masterful series of essays in defense of the US Constitution. Hamilton was writing in a hurry—his main goal was to encourage the New York legislature in its deliberations over whether to ratify the Constitution—and so he began his work in an unlikely place: the cabin of a boat making a journey up the Hudson River from New York to Albany.[1]

Federalist No. 1, which would be published only a few short weeks later, is not typically ranked with the most famous of the eighty-five essays, yet it deserves to be read closely for its relevance to contemporary debates.[2] To Hamilton, the adoption of the US Constitution was about nothing less than determining "whether societies of men are really capable or not of establishing good government from reflection and choice, or whether they are forever destined to depend . . . on accident and force." Hamilton understood that in a vast and diverse country like the United States, it is impossible to reach consensus about each and every political issue—and unwise to resolve arguments by simply letting the side with more power decide.

So what is the alternative to government by force? For Hamilton (and fellow founding fathers James Madison and John Jay, who also contributed to *The Federalist Papers*), a good place to start is by taking humans as they are, as opposed to how we wish they might be.

Concepts that are fundamental to American democracy, like limiting government through the separation of powers and building safeguards to prevent the "tyranny of the majority," are built on the idea that effective governance must be based on bargaining, compromise, and (perhaps most importantly) deep humility. Hamilton understood that "wise and good men" were to be found on the wrong as well as on the right side of any given issue.

Hamilton was particularly concerned about the potential of political factions to inflame passions and undermine the moderation necessary to govern. He bemoaned the "intolerant spirit" that characterized political parties and the "torrent of angry and malignant passions" that accompany partisan efforts to increase converts "by the loudness of their declamations and by the bitterness of their invectives."[3]

This book is written in the spirit of *Federalist No. 1*. We seek to follow Hamilton's lead by making a forceful and unapologetic argument that a gradual and incremental approach to public policy is not only the best way to describe how government actually works, but (almost always) a more effective way of making change happen—even large-scale change.

As Hamilton might have predicted, "a torrent of angry and malignant passions" is a good way to describe our current political moment. Indeed, recent years have been marked by calls for radical change from those on both the right and the left who profoundly distrust the American system of government that has emerged over two centuries after the ratification of the US Constitution.

On the right, Donald Trump waged a successful presidential campaign in 2016 that was animated primarily by an urge for disruption. Every part of Trump's verbal and nonverbal presentation communicated an opposition to politics as usual. His populist message managed to tap into a deep wellspring of discontent among a segment of the electorate that disdained the power and condescension of American educational, cultural, and economic elites.

In a campaign that was light on policy specifics, one of the few promises that Trump made was that he would "drain the swamp" in Washington, DC. This kind of rhetoric, repeated consistently over the course of his four-year presidency, set the stage for the events of January 6, 2021, when a motley crowd of his diehard supporters stormed the Capitol seeking the ultimate in radical change: to overturn Joe Biden's victory in the 2020 presidential election.

On the left, calls for bold change—Green New Deal! Abolish ICE! Defund the Police!—have also been intense and widespread of late. Radical thinkers on the left have pointed to a host of problems with the United States, including the government's failure to address climate change, provide affordable health care for all, and reduce economic inequality. For many on the left, all of these shortcomings (and more besides) are the inevitable and bitter fruit of a poisoned harvest: a country that was founded on the original sins of exploitation and oppression.

America's persistent inability to live up to its founding ideals of freedom and equality, particularly for Black Americans, has been the rocket fuel that has accelerated many left-wing calls for radical change. Ibram X. Kendi, the author of *How to Be an Antiracist* and one of the most prominent American radicals of the moment, makes this explicit when he writes:

> Will Americans support anti-racist policy solutions that match the scale of the problem? Will Americans get big, think big, act big? Big like reparations. Big like basic incomes. Big like defunding the police. Big like Medicare for All. Big like automatic voter registration and online voting. Big like need-based school funding. Big like canceling all student debt. Big like the Green New Deal. Big like racial inequity becoming the marker of racist policy. . . . A century from now, when almost all of us are dead, if we don't act with urgency and boldness, I can only imagine what our descendants will be saying about us. *How could we allow the evil of racial inequity to live another hour? How could we not support a scorched-earth policy to eliminate racial injustice?* The revolutionaries of today will age well, as those revolutionaries of yesterday aged well.[4]

Kendi and other left-wing proponents of radical change are animated by what Martin Luther King Jr. once called "the fierce urgency of now"—and by a hard-earned understanding that, in the United States, the instinct to move with "all deliberate speed" has often meant delay and obstruction on key progressive priorities like school desegregation. A recent essay in *The Atlantic,* entitled "Incremental Change is a Moral Failure," exemplified the radical left perspective. Inside, the author, Mychal Denzel Smith, argues for police abolition and claims that incremental reform "keeps the grinding forces of oppression—of death—in place."

On the right, advocates of radicalism channel the spirit of Barry Goldwater's famous mantra, "Extremism in defense of liberty is no vice. Moderation in pursuit of justice is no virtue." A recent case in point is an article in *Real Clear Politics* decrying the fact that conservatives have "lost control of every important American institution." According to the author, Bruce Abramson, "The GOP has spent decades promoting respectable, cautious incrementalists like Mitch McConnell, John Roberts, and Kevin McCarthy—fine men blessed with none of the skills necessary to lead a counterrevolution."[5]

In short, radical activists on the left and the right don't agree about much of anything these days, but they do seem to share a contempt for incremental reform.[6] Bernie Sanders captured the mindset of both left- and right-wing radicals (appropriately enough, on Twitter) when he declared flatly, "Incremental change is not enough."

But is this correct? Is bold change the only way forward? Are we living in an era that demands the radical transformation of American society?

We don't think so.

Given the widespread calls for radical change, we know that arguments in favor of gradual reform will be greeted with exasperation in some quarters. So before we begin to make the case for incrementalism, we want to anticipate, and cede, a few points that our opponents are likely to make.

1) *We are in fact living through disruptive times.* The digital revolution has transformed the way that we experience the world and we are just beginning to understand the implications. The challenges of adapting to digital life have only been exacerbated by the Covid-19 pandemic. And

all of these dislocations have occurred against a backdrop of declining American engagement in the kinds of civic institutions—churches, clubs, bowling leagues, and the like—that traditionally have helped to bind the country together, a phenomenon that Robert Putnam, of *Bowling Alone* fame, has been documenting for decades. In short, there are good reasons why many people feel out of sorts and unhappy with the status quo these days.

2) *There are big problems in the United States.* There is a great deal of truth to the critiques offered by radical activists on both sides of the aisle. On the left, much of the passion for radical change is driven by racial injustice. Progressive activists are correct when they observe that American descendants of slavery continue to lag behind other Americans in important measures like family wealth and longevity. Economic inequality and climate change are also progressive concerns that warrant serious government action. For their part, right-wing activists are motivated by a sense that they are losing the culture wars. And it is true that many of our most prominent universities have become hostile environments for conservatives and the White working-class. The same goes for leading cultural and media institutions. So radicals on both sides are not just chasing shadows—they are responding to genuine problems.

3) *Radical change has accomplished important things in the past.* In the face of overwhelming opposition, radical left-wing movements in the United States have achieved some remarkable wins. As historian Eric Foner has observed:

Many achievements that we think of as the most admirable in our history are to a considerable extent the outgrowth of American radicalism, including the abolition of slavery, the dramatic expansion of women's rights, the respect for civil liberties and our right of dissent, and the efforts today to tame a rampant capitalism and combat economic inequality. Many of our current ideas about freedom, equality, and the rights of citizens originated with American radicals.[7]

As good liberals ourselves, we are less sanguine about the impacts of right-wing radicalism in this country. But even we can acknowledge that the Reagan revolution did reshape our country in significant ways (and that not all of those impacts were bad).

Our argument is not that radical change is never possible or desirable. Extraordinary historical moments—World War II, the Great Depression, the Civil Rights Movement—have indeed required bold governmental solutions. (Of course, it must also be said that when government moves quickly to implement radical change, it often leaves blood in the streets—as in Mao's China, Hitler's Germany, and Stalin's Russia.)

But we do not believe that we are living through times that necessitate radical change. It is true that our country has serious problems to address, but that has always been the case. What's different today is not the nature or extent of our problems, but the way that our media environment encourages catastrophizing by anyone who wants to advance a policy idea or a social reform. It often seems that the only way to be heard above the din is to scream louder than everybody else. As journalist Matthew Yglesias writes:

> There are a lot of writers around these days propagating a fundamentally false and unsubstantiated notion that we are living through some acute "global social, political, and economic crises." . . . I think [this] crisis-mongering outlook is fundamentally illiberal and harmful. . . . I would say that we are living through some problems that are both serious and difficult, but not necessarily any more serious or more difficult than the problems of the past . . . mostly I think we're living through a time of toxic self-involved drama that threatens to make things worse through twitchy overreaction.[8]

To which we say: amen.

In this book, we hope to tamp down the rampant crisis-mongering and to help separate the signal from the noise. One of the biggest problems facing the world at the moment is that there is simply more noise than ever before. As Martin Gurri argues in *The Revolt of the Public*, humanity is suffering from profound information overload.

He points out that more information was generated in 2001 than in all of the previous existence of our species on earth: "In fact, 2001 *doubled* the previous total. And 2002 doubled the amount present in 2001."[9]

Twenty years into the millennium, we are light years away from the world that many of us grew up in, where most Americans got their information from their local newspaper and Walter Cronkite. Today we are awash in information graphics, TikTok dances, blogs, Instagram photos, cell phone videos, and much, much more. Who could possibly make sense of it all?

It may seem counterintuitive, but gradualism is particularly well suited to our current moment and a world in which a shared sense of reality has fractured. Far from being a "moral failure," incremental reform is in fact the best way to address social problems in a climate where it is difficult to agree on basic facts, let alone expensive, large-scale government interventions.

What are the alternatives to gradualism? For some people, the answer is that government should do nothing. But even those who are completely satisfied with the status quo should recognize that change is inescapable. As Giuseppe Lampedusa, the Italian author of *The Leopard*, once wrote: "If we want things to stay as they are, things will have to change."

Others advance utopian schemes, such as prison or police abolition, that generate buzz on the internet but have almost no chance of real-world implementation.

But perhaps the most seductive alternative to gradual change is what Charles Lindblom, a political science professor at Yale and one of the leading theorists of incrementalism, called the "synoptic" approach, which seeks to fashion comprehensive solutions to problems, often driven by centralized planners. The fundamental weakness of this approach is that it requires access to high-quality information, agreement about underlying values, and effective decision-making on the part of government planners. In the real world, these conditions rarely, if ever, exist. Much more common are the opposite: bad data, furiously competing interests, and flawed decision makers subject to the same cognitive biases as the rest of us.

There are numerous advantages to gradual reform, in contrast to utopianism and comprehensive planning. Instead of pursuing broad, revolutionary change in a single master stroke, incrementalism focuses on addressing concrete problems in a piecemeal fashion. Following the scientific method, incremental reform allows for new ideas to be tested, evaluated, and honed over time. Learning by trial and error is essential because the world is complex and full of conflicting interests.

Crucially, gradualists know how little they know. Anyone trying to understand a given problem these days is necessarily missing crucial information because there is simply too much information to process effectively. Gradualists acknowledge that, inevitably, errors happen. Building on this insight, an iterative, incremental process allows for each successive generation of reformers to learn from, and improve upon, their predecessors' efforts.

Critics of incrementalism often argue that it is timid or slow or a de facto endorsement of the status quo. But experience indicates that small changes, compounded over time, can add up to something significant. As Harvard psychologist Steven Pinker has highlighted, modest improvements, accumulating over many generations, have led to dramatic reductions in the rates of global violence, poverty, and mortality, improving the quality of life for hundreds of millions of people.

While some gradual improvements take decades, incrementalism is also, paradoxically, capable of delivering quick results. According to Daniel Herriges of the nonprofit Strong Towns: "Incrementalism entails a bias toward quick action over exhaustive planning: you take the next, easiest action to address the immediate situation you're facing, and you take it right now. You don't wait to have the whole road map to your policy goal laid out for you."[10]

Moreover, incrementalism has the virtue of being democratic. The goal of incremental change is typically to encourage experimentation, to let a thousand flowers bloom, rather than insisting that there is only one true path to change and attempting to exercise centralized control of its implementation.

Unfortunately, incrementalism has become unfashionable at the precise moment when we need it most. Writing in 1955, French philosopher Raymond Aron bemoaned the fact that the outcomes of incremental reform can be "as boring as an English Sunday."[11] Social media has only made the problem worse. Thanks in no small part to Twitter and Facebook, our political conversation at the moment seems to veer wildly between two poles—expressions of hopelessness (e.g., climate despair, Afropessimism) and advocacy for disruptive agendas that have little chance of implementation in real life (e.g., calls for implementing socialism and passing the Green New Deal or closing our borders and withdrawing from NATO).

In writing this book, we seek to shift this dynamic, arguing that gradualism offers us a sensible way forward, that even small successes should be celebrated because they are enormously difficult to achieve, and that, over time, incremental reforms can add up to something truly transformative.

In making the case for the virtues of incrementalism, this book is organized into three sections:

Section I: A World of Constraints

First, we outline the real-world considerations that make radical change difficult in the American context. Each of the three chapters in this section is devoted to exploring a different myth that is often advanced by radical activists. We begin in Chapter 1, "Muddling Through," by addressing the widely held perception that the partisan animosities of recent years have resulted in a broken, endlessly gridlocked Congress. Instead, we show how Congress, while by no means perfect, continues to work in much the way that the American founders envisioned. Under the radar, Democrats and Republicans have continued to forge bipartisan legislation to advance important goals, even during the hyper-polarized Trump years.[12]

In Chapter 2, "The Practitioner Veto," we examine the belief that electoral victories can be easily translated into changes in government practice on the ground. The reality is more complicated. Of course political victories matter. Even in a system like ours that is designed to limit the powers of government, elections have consequences. But there is an underappreciated brake on even the most powerful of elected officials: government workers, including the street-level bureaucrats closest to the ground, have minds of their own. They can and will subvert new programs and new policies that have been imposed on them without their consent. In the end, public policy comes down to implementation, and the realities of implementation, of how hard it is to actually do things differently and to improve outcomes even marginally, will almost always end up tilting government toward incrementalism.

In Chapter 3, "What the Public Wants," we take on the claim that the American public is hungering for bold change. Reviewing the data from dozens of public opinion polls, including one that we commissioned specifically for this book, we find that the American public is more interested in incremental reform than radical transformation. Encouragingly, while certain kinds of political polarization have increased in recent years, there is nonetheless fairly broad public support for a range of substantive reforms that have the potential, if enacted, to address some of the social problems that continue to bedevil us.

Section II: Incrementalism in Action

In this section, we share a few stories of what successful incrementalism looks like in practice. We begin with the story of Social Security. In the popular imagination, the New Deal is often conceived of as a series of revolutionary changes that were implemented by arguably the most powerful American president ever, Franklin Delano

Roosevelt, to deal with the devastating economic hardship wrought by the Great Depression. While much of this story is true, a closer look reveals that the creation of the Social Security Administration— one of our largest, most durable, and most politically popular government institutions—does not hew to this narrative. Social Security was largely the product of two cautious, behind-the-scenes reformers from Wisconsin who intentionally chose to develop the program in an incremental fashion when there were more radical and comprehensive options on the table.

Chapter 5 offers a case study in what we call "accidental incrementalism." A generation ago, New York City's jail population ballooned to more than 22,000, and the city seemed stuck in a downward spiral of soaring crime rates and ever-expanding incarceration. Today, New York is in a very different place. Even after a rise in shootings during the pandemic, it is still one of the safest big cities in the country and it has fewer than 5,500 people in jail. One of the striking things about New York City's jail population is that it has gone down almost every year since 1989. No single policy change sparked the decline. Instead, a series of mostly unheralded innovations—what *New Yorker* writer Adam Gopnik has called "a thousand small sanities"—set the wheels in motion. The reduced use of incarceration in New York City is a case study of how years of gradual improvement can add up to sweeping change.

In Chapter 6, we tell a different kind of incremental success story, looking at one of the most controversial issues in American politics: immigration. The history of immigration policy in the United States is messy, ugly, and rife with racism—for decades, immigrants from "White" countries were explicitly favored over immigrants from non-White nations. Yet, for all of its flaws, American immigration policy has also helped fuel much of the social, cultural, and economic dynamism of this country. For us, immigration policy is an example of what we would label "hidden incrementalism." When it has worked best, it has done so out of the spotlight of public and political scrutiny. The American approach is also oriented to immigrant self-selection rather than top-down identification of particularly desirable immigrants, which offers distinct benefits as well.

Section III: Stumbling toward Success

In our final section, we attempt to flesh out the contours of a brand of gradualism that meets our current moment. We begin by examining an effort by the federal government to advance sweeping change: the "Great Society" program put forth by President Lyndon Baines Johnson. In particular, we look at two anti-poverty programs, Community Action and Model Cities, that struggled to achieve their goals despite being launched with great fanfare (and a significant infusion of federal money). We argue that these programs are examples of failed incrementalism; many of the problems they encountered can be attributed to moving too big, too fast.

Despite the demonstrable success of the incremental approach, it remains highly unpopular in many quarters. We examine the reasons for this as prelude to articulating our own brand of gradualism. In Chapter 8, we highlight four core elements of incrementalism—honesty, humility, nuance, and respect. We explain how each of these values is under threat at the moment, and how they might be defended going forward.

We conclude our book with a rumination on Amara's Law. This is the idea, named after Stanford computer scientist Roy Amara, that people fall into the trap of overestimating what can be accomplished in the short term and underestimating what can be accomplished in the long term. It is usually hard to see progress happening in the moment. But if we can just take a step back and use a longer time horizon, it often becomes apparent that significant change has happened. By observing Amara's Law, we can avoid the disappointment that inevitably comes from living in a world of overinflated expectations.

★ ★ ★

We have written this book because we believe that developing a keener appreciation for the value of gradualism is crucial to the future success of the United States. Yet we acknowledge our limitations in making this case. We are not historians. Nor are we philosophers. Others are better placed than we are to trace the origins of incrementalism or to explain how gradual reform in the United States compares to gradual reform in other countries. We hope in the days ahead that other writers will build on the arguments that we have sketched within these pages and take our thinking to the next level.

We have written this book in a spirit of forward-looking, pragmatic optimism. We hope it will serve as a call to arms for the millions of Americans who are turned off by the overheated rhetoric, gloomy outlook, and unrealistic aspirations that characterize so much of political discourse in the social media era.

Why are large segments of the American public so pessimistic? In 2013, the Swedish public health expert Hans Rosling began asking people a fundamental question about global poverty: has the percentage of the world population that lives in extreme poverty almost doubled, almost halved, or stayed the same over the past twenty years? Only 5 percent of Americans got the right answer: extreme poverty has been cut almost in half. A chimpanzee, picking answers at random, would do much better. Looking at Rosling's efforts, Matt Ridley, the author of *The Rational Optimist*, concludes: "People are worse than ignorant: They believe they know many dire things about the world that are, in fact, untrue."[13]

According to Ridley, one of the reasons for our predilection for pessimism is simple: bad news is more sudden than good news, which is usually gradual. As a result, the bad things that happen in the world are significantly more memorable than positive developments.

Our interest in incrementalism—and our optimism—is informed by our real-life experience attempting to advance change within the American criminal justice system. The two of us first met in 1999, when we both were working at the Center for Court Innovation, a nonprofit organization dedicated to promoting a more fair, effective, and humane justice system through research and demonstration programs.

During the fifteen years we spent working together there, the Center for Court Innovation assisted thousands of judges, attorneys, probation officials, police officers, and other frontline practitioners who were interested in reforming the justice system from within. We saw up close how difficult this work can be. Government agencies are remarkably resistant to change. Like silly putty, no matter how much you poke and pull at them, if you step away for even a moment, they tend to return to the status quo ante. We also saw reform efforts go sideways, which inspired us to write our first book together, *Trial & Error in Criminal Justice Reform: Learning from Failure*. So we understand why many are pessimistic about the possibilities of progress.

On the flip side, we have also seen just how many of the people who toil within government are laboring to do the right thing in exceedingly challenging circumstances—working with limited information and inadequate resources to solve seemingly intractable problems. This work should be honored, not denigrated.

We have also seen that small changes can make a big difference. Just as compound interest can, over time, add up to significant wealth, so too can seemingly minor improvements in government outcomes generate massive improvements in the quality of life for millions of people. A 10 percent reduction in recidivism in a given program may not sound like much, but if the program is able to sustain those reductions over enough years, it will have a demonstrable impact on public safety.

Since leaving the Center for Court Innovation, we have gone on to other positions in other settings, but the lessons we learned have stayed with us: change is hard. Many government workers are doing the best they can. And small improvements, over time, add up to something substantial.

Of course, no one has a crystal ball capable of predicting which small reforms will eventually pay big dividends. The world is too contingent and complex for this to be possible. It is also true that not every change is a step forward—progress is, in fact, reversible. But we believe that, barring some extraordinary event or cataclysm, it is neither possible nor desirable to skip over the hard slog of making change happen step-by-step in incremental fashion.

Earlier, we admitted that radical change, particularly the left-wing variety, has been responsible for some of the most important achievements in American history. But the track record of gradualism is just as powerful, if not more so.

In recent days, the two of us have, at various points, taken a subway ride, sat in a local park, drunk clean water from a tap, and visited a public library. The streets we walked on were, by and large, clean and safe. No policeman approached us looking for a bribe. All of these building blocks of a good life can be traced back, in one way or another, to incremental improvements by government. If we can just manage to keep our faith in gradual reform, who knows what we might achieve in the years to come?

SECTION I

A World of
Constraints

I

Muddling Through

In 2019, Princeton political scientist Frances E. Lee appeared on a popular podcast hosted by uber-policy geek Ezra Klein, the cofounder of the website *Vox*. Klein had invited Lee to talk about her book, *Insecure Majorities: Congress and the Perpetual Campaign*. According to Klein, "It's not often I run across political science that genuinely changes my understanding of how American politics works. . . . Frances Lee's research has done exactly that."[1]

Lee thinks that the intensifying partisanship of American politics can be traced to greater electoral competition at the federal level in recent years. With the exception of just four years, Democrats controlled the House and Senate from 1933 to 1980. They also held the presidency for two-thirds of this time. But since then, control of Congress and the presidency has swung back and forth between the two parties. For the minority party, denying the governing party high-profile victories has become a rational strategy for regaining power. This idea was exemplified by Senate Majority Leader Mitch McConnell's (in)famous statement about his top legislative priorities for 2010: "The single most important thing we want to achieve is for President Obama to be a one-term president."[2]

As a result of all of this "constant, intense competition," Lee told Klein, "politicians are continually preoccupied with politics (and) with their ability to hold on to power, with messaging, with their image as opposed to being able to think about what they actually want to do with power."[3]

At first glance, Lee's take appears to reinforce a widely shared narrative about American political decline—that politicians are dithering while the world burns, focused on their short-term personal ambitions at the cost of solving real problems. This message has been repeated so often in the media that it has essentially become an echo chamber: A *New York Times* headline reads "As Gridlock Deepens in Congress, Only Gloom Is Bipartisan."[4] For the *Washington Post,* it's "Gridlock in Congress? It's Probably Even Worse Than You Think."[5] Not to be outdone, *Vox* reports that "Hyperpartisanship could destroy US democracy," positing a "frightening 'doom loop' of mutual distrust."[6]

Only toward the end of Klein's podcast does it become clear that Lee does not share this nihilistic view. While she admits that gridlock is usually an accurate way to describe "the issues of highest salience in American politics," Lee argues that American government "isn't inoperative a lot of the time, it's just not resolving the issues that those of us who follow politics . . . want to see." Indeed, "for most of the time, government is functioning tolerably well."

Government is easily underestimated these days. According to Lee, "If issues can fly below the radar, if they're not seen as a test of a President's performance, then more progress is possible, sometimes even on very contentious issues." She cited the 2016 Toxic Substances Act, a piece of legislation that (after a decade of bipartisan negotiation) resulted in a major expansion of the Environmental Protection Agency, as a case in point.

It is probably fair to say that very few of the listeners to Klein's podcast had ever heard of the Toxic Substances Act. You could almost hear the record scratching as Lee mentioned the legislation, which enabled the EPA to regulate over 80,000 additional chemicals used by private business. The Toxic Substances Act might be obscure, but it is "likely the greatest delegation of authority by Congress and the President to the EPA in four decades" according to one scholar.[7]

Environmental regulation is hardly uncontroversial, which begs the questions: why has no one heard of the 2016 Toxic Substances

Act? Is this the exception that proves the rule of partisan gridlock? Or does it suggest that perhaps the media echo chamber is wrong about the extent to which government dysfunction haunts this country?

Secret Congress

In attempting to answer these questions, it might be useful to find a physical copy of the May 20, 2021, edition of the *New York Times*. An above-the-fold, front-page story documents the collapse of a bipartisan agreement to investigate the January 6, 2021, assault on the US Capitol. "Some Democrats," the article reads, "said the episode only underscored to them that it was pointless to negotiate with the Republicans on any of the big issues that divide the parties."[8]

The article opens to an inside page, where it shares space with a shorter article at the bottom entitled "Bipartisan Bill Aims to Rescue Postal Service." This less prominent article details the work of a bipartisan group to help the Postal Service deal with its crippling financial crisis. The article calls the negotiation an "indication of bipartisan compromise in a divided Congress."[9]

As Lee suggests, this dynamic plays itself out over and over again in American politics: on the kinds of issues that make it to the front page of the *New York Times*, it is impossible for Democrats and Republicans to agree. On the kinds of issues that are buried in the less well-read, internal pages of the newspaper, bipartisan agreement happens all of the time. Blogger Matthew Yglesias has a label for this below-the-radar collaborative work: "Secret Congress."

Lee has attempted to document the activities of Secret Congress. After writing *Insecure Majorities*, she worked with James M. Curry of the University of Utah to examine Congress's ability to pass legislation from 1985 to 2018. The method they used borrowed from Yale University political scientist David Mayhew's classic book *Divided We Govern*. Lee and Curry identified 265 key legislative priorities

articulated by the leadership of the majority party in the House
and the Senate during each two-year Congressional session. They
wanted to know how effective majority parties have been at realizing
their most important priorities. Or to put the question another way:
how well does Congress perform its primary function—successfully
passing legislation?

Lee and Curry's findings echoed Mayhew's earlier research: majority parties were able to successfully pass their priority legislation
about half of the time. Not great, but not exactly an argument that
Congress does nothing. Strikingly, when important laws did pass, they
typically did so with large bipartisan majorities—much like the 2016
Toxic Substances Act, which passed the House by a 403–13 vote and
by voice vote in the Senate (a voice vote doesn't require a tally of individual voters).

In Lee and Curry's analysis, there were only nine instances where
the majority party "steamrolled" the opposing party by passing legislation in a completely partisan fashion. By contrast, they documented fifty-two instances where legislative priorities passed with
bipartisan support, and an additional seventy-four where party
leaders watered down their original proposal to get support from
the other side. In other words, compromise and consensus is the
typical pattern in Congress, as opposed to unilateral action. "At the
broadest level, this research reveals that Congress has not changed
nearly as much as it is often assumed," Lee and Curry write. "Much
about congressional lawmaking remains the same, despite the tre-
mendous rise of partisan conflict and the empowering of party
leadership."[10]

"When we first started presenting the findings, we got a lot of
surprise and disbelief," Curry says. "It's hard for people to accept
in today's media." For Lee, this skepticism is a sign of how political parties have excelled at making the public believe there is no
common ground between them. "They do that so successfully,"
Lee says, "that most Americans aren't aware that legislating is still
bipartisan."

When Theory Meets Reality

For Lee, the ultimate lesson is that "theory often gets in the way of people understanding how the world really works. When the system doesn't match the theory," she says, "then they want to dismantle the system. It's appealing to imagine that you can remake public policy according to a grand vision. That's certainly how a party campaigns."

Curry adds that, in the interviews they conducted, Congressional insiders make it clear that they understand how the game is really played. "Those folks . . . recognize differences between messaging and legislating," Curry says. "One staffer told me, 'the dumbest thing you can do is try to pass a bill without support from the other side.'"[II]

This hasn't stopped many pundits, including Klein, from arguing that Congress is fundamentally broken. In recent years, a number of significant structural changes have been mooted, particularly by left-leaning critics frustrated with Congress's failure to enact sweeping legislation like the Green New Deal or Medicare for All. These include eliminating the filibuster, abolishing the Electoral College, packing the Supreme Court, and advancing statehood for Washington, DC, and Puerto Rico, among other ideas.

According to Mayhew, the impulse to change congressional procedures goes back to the late nineteenth century and Woodrow Wilson. Before becoming president, Wilson was a prominent political scientist. He raised difficult questions about the inability of the fragmented American political system to respond sufficiently to urgent public concerns. What Wilson sought was something akin to the British parliamentary system, in which government majorities are broadly empowered to enact their legislative priorities. Wilson was ultimately unsuccessful, though as president, he did preside over a significant expansion of the power of the executive branch.

In the 1950s, a number of political scientists advanced a "strong party" theory of change. They believed that greater ideological distinction between the two major American political parties would benefit voters by giving them a clearer choice at the ballot box. At the time, the Democratic Party combined a northern, liberal faction with a southern faction that regularly blocked civil rights legislation. On the Republican side, liberal "Rockefeller Republicans" jockeyed for influence with more conservative voices.

The strong party theory sought to clarify this messy political reality. Proponents of the theory argued that a combination of more centralized leadership and greater internal party cohesion would lead to greater congressional output, because it would give majority parties the freedom and discipline to pass their legislative priorities. Voters would be better able to identify parties with their policy priorities and, over time, reward those parties whose policies had a more positive impact.[12]

Since then, American political parties have indeed become much more cohesive ideologically. And congressional leadership has grown more centralized. Despite these developments, little has changed in terms of congressional legislation. The strong party theory appears not to have worked. So, rinse and repeat, as the failure of one theory begets a new round of calls for fundamental change based on different theories. According to Mayhew, when the policy aims of a given party falter on Capitol Hill, "There must be a reason. Culprit processes are found. It is a short step to the view: 'My party can't get what it wants, so the system must be broken.'"[13]

What to Expect When You're (Not) Expecting

At the root of the debate about whether government is hopelessly gridlocked or about as functional as ever is another important question: just how much should we expect from government? If we start out with low expectations, then what government is able to accomplish looks pretty good. High expectations lead to the opposite conclusion.

The fundamental conflict appears to be whether one is an idealist or realist about the American political system. Mayhew, Lee, and Curry are in the realist camp. "A diverse public will help stop wild change," says Curry. "Our (legislative) system forces us to build consensus." For Lee, one virtue of our political system is that it "fragments power" between different branches of government and at various levels (federal, state, local). The result is that "both parties have a stake in the system and their supporters are represented in different ways."[14]

A recent example of the fragmentation of authority in the United States is the decision by twenty-five Republican governors to end federal unemployment benefits months before the September 2021 deadline set by the Biden administration.[15] This is not an isolated example—governors and mayors often look for ways to opt out of federal initiatives, particularly when the opposing party occupies the White House. (Think of the "sanctuary city" movement during the Trump administration.)

In our federal system, many of the most contentious issues resist resolution. There is rarely a definitive victory for one side over the other. Instead, the fight typically grinds on, waged on multiple fronts simultaneously, with no uniform or comprehensive settlement possible. As frustrating as this may be, it might be the best outcome we can expect when the population is deeply divided about a given issue.

Incrementalism is the lubricant that oils the machinery of American government, allowing the entire Rube Goldberg contraption to keep lurching forward, however fitfully. Incrementalism allows government decision makers to move away from what is disliked or dysfunctional, even (or especially) when they cannot come to an agreement on exactly where they are headed. Almost all of the actors within the system are incrementalists in practice, even if they are reluctant to articulate incrementalism as an overarching political philosophy.

Indeed, one of the essential roles played by an institution like Congress is to resist change that does not have overwhelming public support. In a provocative passage in his book *The Imprint of Congress*, Mayhew notes that "inaction as well as action can be legitimizing":

Often, when confronted by a polarized, dissonant, or irresolute public the unsurprising behavior of a representative assembly is to do nothing at all. Often, when Congress is doing nothing at all, to the despair of partisans, intellectuals, and the media, it is actually responding to an unresolved electorate with a perfect ear. *Don't!* the public is in effect collectively saying. Consider a stark counterfactual: Every quick, narrow, temporary majority gets to jam into law whatever its activist base wants. Play that out for awhile, especially in a context of ideological polarization, and what level of system legitimacy would result?[16]

The founders of the American constitutional system were realists. They sought to create a government structure that could manage and productively direct conflict and disagreement. The idea was to encourage competing power centers within the growing American nation. As James Madison wrote in *Federalist No. 51*, "Ambition must be made to counteract ambition."

The Constitution itself serves as a good example of the contested reality of American government. The product of a kludgy, messy debate that satisfied none of the protagonists—let alone critics today—it has nonetheless stood the test of time, while allowing for continuous revision and reinterpretation over more than two centuries.

In his book *Madison's Metronome*, the political scientist Greg Weiner argues that James Madison's core principle was gradualism. While Madison is typically understood as seeking to prevent the "tyranny of the majority," Weiner offers a slightly different image of the founding father who served as the fourth president of the United States. He suggests that Madison was a realist who knew that majorities would eventually prevail in the end. But, according to Weiner, Madison's goal was to encourage majorities to take their time before imposing their policy preferences—what he calls a "seasoned majority."

Madison's commitment to gradualism is best seen in an exchange of letters with Thomas Jefferson in 1789, in which Jefferson famously urged Madison to make the Constitution fully renewable every two decades, so that the next generation of government decision makers would not be bound by outdated rules set by their predecessors. In his reply, Madison pushed back firmly. He warned against sudden change and putting too much faith in human rationality, writing, "we must perceive the necessity of moderating still further our expectations and hopes from the efforts of human sagacity." By cultivating patience, Madison thought that government officials might have the advantage of seeing issues across time rather than making judgments in the passion of the moment.[17]

As Madison makes plain, it all comes down to expectations. For realists, the slow pace of government change is a product of the fragmented nature of American government and the trade-offs required to reach consensus across a diverse society. From this perspective, any kind of reform, even modest ones, should be appreciated as a hard-fought victory. For idealists, however, it is difficult to celebrate modest victories or to acknowledge gradual progress when there is so much injustice still to address.

Budgeting Is Incremental

The divide between idealists and realists doesn't just play out in lofty debates over the American Constitution. It is also reflected in the nitty-gritty details of how government officials carry out their day-to-day tasks.

Here again, incrementalism oils the machine.

Perhaps the best way to develop an appreciation of the way incrementalism is built into everyday government activity is to start with Aaron Wildavsky. The founding dean of the Graduate School for Public Policy at the University of California–Berkeley, Wildavsky was the first academic to give serious attention to government budgeting, a curious omission given the critical importance of the budgetary process—what government chooses to fund, or not fund, is typically the best barometer of its true priorities.

Wildavsky's method was to talk directly with the officials who were central to the federal budgetary process. With a colleague, he spent six weeks in Washington, "interviewing from morning and night. We were not certain whether it was encouraging to discover that no academic investigator had ever spoken to these important people about the work before."[18] The book that came out of his interviews was an intensive study of the federal budget called *The Politics of the Budgetary Process*, originally published in 1964 (three subsequent editions were released, the last in 1984).

Wildavsky's central insight was that "budgeting is incremental, not comprehensive." The best predictor of what will go into any given budget is what went into it last year, with "special attention given to the narrow range of increases or decreases." As Wildavsky memorably wrote, the "budget might be conceived of as an iceberg with by far the largest part below the surface, outside of the control of anyone."[19]

Wildavsky favorably contrasts incrementalism to a more idealized, comprehensive approach to budgeting. As he points out, the demands of such an approach would be overwhelming, both in cognitive and political terms. Deciding on whether a single program is effective is hard enough, but attempting to do so across multiple programs and disparate policy areas on an annual basis would be a herculean task. The budgetary process is fundamentally political—there is no "neutral" process for resolving disputes over the allocation of resources. Creating such a process would represent "the end of conflict over the government's role in society"—an obviously unrealistic aspiration.[20]

By contrast, the incremental approach has a number of concrete benefits. Most important, it reduces decision-making to a smaller and easier set of options. It also minimizes conflict by lowering the stakes of negotiations and enables ongoing learning, giving government officials the chance to allow experience to accumulate. It is worth quoting Wildavsky at length here about the virtues of budgetary incrementalism:

The incremental, fragmented, non-programmatic, and sequential procedures of the present budgetary process aid in securing agreement and
reducing the burden of calculation. It is much easier to agree on an
addition or a reduction of a few thousand or a million than to agree on
whether a program is good in the abstract. It is much easier to agree on
a small addition or decrease than to compare the worth of one program
to that of all others. . . . Finally, agreement comes much more readily
when the items in dispute can be treated as differences in dollars instead
of basic differences in policy.[21]

A big chunk of *The Politics of the Budgetary Process* is given over to a
description of how budget negotiations in government play out in
practice, not in theory. Spenders have three goals, Wildavsky writes:
defending their agency's base of funding from cuts, increasing the
size of the base by enlarging legacy programs, and expanding the
base by proposing new ones. Expecting that the budget guardians
who staff the Office of Management and Budget will trim their
budget requests, spenders are often incentivized to ask for more
than they can reasonably expect to get. Of course, by asking for
too much, they run the risk of eroding their credibility. Likewise,
budget guardians understand that they can cut only so much, especially if a program is favored by powerful legislators or the president.
The result is an intricate dance than unfolds over time in a series of
negotiations.

Anyone with actual experience of the budgeting process will smile
in recognition at this description. As Wildavsky makes plain, incrementalism is not just an easier way to get things done, but a way of
describing a relationship between participants in a negotiation, who
are given specific, defined roles and a relatively narrow range of discretion to carry out their work.

In painting a realistic picture of the budgetary process, Wildavsky
sought to "deal with real men in the real world for whom the best they
can get is to be preferred to the perfection they cannot achieve." (In
Wildavsky's time, budgeting was mostly a male domain.) He pithily
defines an incrementalist as someone who is "unwilling or unable to

alter the basic features of the political system" and who "seeks to make it work for them . . . rather than against them."[22]

Why Comprehensive Reforms Fail

One of the pleasures of reading *The Politics of the Budgetary Process* is how, in each successive edition, Wildavsky knocks down the latest, faddish proposal to reform the budgetary process. This includes program budgeting, management by objectives, and zero-based budgeting (introduced by President Jimmy Carter), which sought to set all budgets back to zero, establish priorities across government, and reallocate dollars to the highest priorities—even if that meant ending incumbent programs.

Each case study follows a familiar narrative: an unrealistic attempt to wrestle the messy and incremental process of budgeting into a more comprehensive and "rational" approach. "All that is accomplished by injunctions to follow a comprehensive approach," Wildavsky writes, "is the inculcation of guilt among good men who find that they can never come close to fulfilling this unreasonable expectation. Worse still, acceptance of an unreasonable goal inhibits discussion of the methods actually used."[23]

These failed attempts at comprehensive reform, therefore, end up looking a lot like the strong party theory that political scientists mistakenly believed would allow government to act more freely and provide voters more clarity about their choices as they went to the ballot box, or Jefferson's advocacy for starting the Constitution over from scratch every two decades. Each of these efforts makes some sense in the abstract, while failing miserably in practice.

If there is one idea that serves as the intellectual foundation for incrementalism, it's that human beings, who always face severe cognitive, conceptual, and political constraints, cannot operate according to a comprehensive ideal. Instead, they take shortcuts and seek to reduce their decision-making burden into manageable chunks. They do so not out of an excessive fealty to the status quo but because it is the best way to actually get things done in the real world.

One of the core appeals of incrementalism is that it allows us to face the world as it really is, as opposed to its idealized form. It also encourages humility about how much change is possible or desirable given limited information and uncertainty about the impact of our actions. The most common critique of incrementalism—that it is effectively a concession to an unjust status quo—gets it exactly backward. Much of politics is an attempt to get the world to conform to a preexisting idea of how it should operate in the face of overwhelming facts to the contrary. The inability, or unwillingness, to alter one's approach in the face of reality is the standard operating procedure for many political activists across the spectrum. The economist Albert Hirschman, a key incremental thinker, captured this dynamic perfectly: "It is the poverty of our imagination that paradoxically produces images of 'total' change in lieu of more modest expectations."[24]

"I Call It Progress"

If there is a foundational text for American incrementalism, it is probably Charles Lindblom's 1959 article "The Science of Muddling Through." For Lindblom, a professor of political science who taught at Yale for nearly forty years, the chief virtue of incrementalism is that it starts with the understanding that "making policy is at best a very rough process":

> Neither social scientists, nor politicians, nor public administrators yet know enough about the social world to avoid repeated error in predicting the consequences of policy moves. A wise policy-maker consequently expects that his policies will achieve only part of what he hopes and at the same time will produce unintended consequences he would have preferred to avoid. If he proceeds through a succession of incremental changes, he avoids serious lasting mistakes in several ways.[25]

To Lindblom, this more constrained way of approaching public policy is not a failure of imagination "for which administrators ought to apologize," but a vibrant and defensible method of its own.

Many pieces of congressional legislation follow a gradual path to completion. The 2016 Toxic Substances Act provides a good example of this process. It is an update to legislation, passed in 1976, that quickly proved to be anemic: poorly drafted and implemented, it enabled only a few hundred potentially toxic chemicals to be tested.

Despite these evident failures, many observers doubted the legislation would ever be revisited. And then the circumstances changed: the passage of more stringent regulations by the European Union and state officials in California in 2007 and 2008 left the chemical industry in a position where they wanted national regulation to preempt state rules and be in alignment with international requirements.

Even with these incentives to act, negotiations over the legislation took over a decade to come to completion. It took so long that the bill's original sponsor, Senator Frank Lautenberg, died before the law was passed; in 2014, retiring congressman John Dingell, another important protagonist, said, "This is a piece of legislation that has sat around and I think will probably sit around until hell freezes over."

The reason for this delay was the delicate balancing act between the chemical industry and environmental groups. "Constructing a statute that would be politically acceptable to such diverse interests built in more hurdles that if it was simply authored by a policy analyst or enlightened social planner," writes Stanford political scientist Lawrence S. Rothenberg in *Policy Success in an Age of Gridlock*. He sees the passage of the Toxic Substances Act as a model for other potential major legislative reforms when the interests of industry and environmental groups coincide (such as encouraging consumers to buy electronic vehicles), while acknowledging that these underlying conditions are not often met.

Another feature of the 2016 Toxic Substances Act worth noting is that it was an update of a preexisting law. While this is a rational approach for incrementalists to take, it poses legitimate public policy challenges, because many original laws are arguably not fit for purpose.

Rothenberg credits a small number of legislators and representatives of industry and environmental groups with getting the 2016 Toxic Substances Act across the finish line. He notes that its passage cannot be attributed to a major environmental catastrophe, as in the example of the Superfund program following the Love Canal disaster.[26]

As we will see throughout this book, the ability to move forward in the face of complexity is a crucial element of incrementalism. Just ask Democratic senator Thomas Carper of Delaware. In a *New York Times* article about the prospects for meaningful climate change legislation soon after President Joe Biden's inauguration in 2021, Senator Carper reeled off a long list of modest programs that had historically attracted bipartisan support that he was itching to sneak into larger pieces of legislation. "You may call it incrementalism," Senator Carper told the *Times*, "but I call it progress."[27]

As Carper's combative quote illustrates, incrementalism is often a tough sell these days. Very few audiences want to hear that the world is more complex than they think and that they should lower their expectations if they hope to accomplish anything.

By contrast, the comprehensive viewpoint has an intuitive appeal, but it offers a false sense of control. As the philosopher Michael Oakeshott has written, it's a lot easier to give the appearance of certainty about a theory than about practical experience, which is always unfolding in unpredictable ways. For Oakeshott, theorizing is like reading a cookbook as opposed to actual cooking. In a resonant phrase, Oakeshott warns us not to put ideas in our heads but no "tastes in our mouths." The downside of many contemporary media accounts of American politics, which often assume that it is only procedural rules that keep Congress from taking more dramatic action, is that they confine themselves to reading the cookbook as opposed to learning how food is prepared in reality.[28]

Incrementalism's PR Problem

Aaron Wildavsky was one academic who was determined to put tastes in his mouth. Perhaps this is one reason why, at the start of his professional career, Wildavsky struggled to gain acceptance. His book was rejected by nine publishers. Even budget officials (the source of much of the information in his book) distanced themselves from it. In his 1974 edition, Wildavsky wrote that "at first the reaction in the old BOB (Bureau of the Budget) was that none of it was true. After about two years the word was that some of it was true. By the time four years had elapsed the line was that most of it was true, but wasn't it a shame." As one scholar recently wrote, "it seemed that budgeting was what it was, not what some might wish it to be."[29]

The gap between how often incrementalism is practiced—versus how often it is openly acknowledged—has been with us for a long time. In his history of Thomas Jefferson's decades-long attempt to establish the University of Virginia, Alan Taylor recounts how Jefferson went to the Virginia legislature for "six or seven successive sessions for aid for the University." According to Taylor, when asked why he didn't just apply for all of the needed money at once, "Jefferson explained that he had learned how to manage legislators by working incrementally." When his strategy was revealed in the *Richmond Enquirer*, Jefferson complained furiously, arguing that his private conversation had been misrepresented. As Taylor notes, Jefferson was protesting too much, for he had successfully "drawn legislators along step by halting step . . . (he) did so shrewdly, (and) persistently." The problem, of course, is that Jefferson didn't want the legislature to know what he was doing.[30]

Jefferson's campaign to establish the University of Virginia and Wildavsky's work on budgeting offer us two examples of the perverse appeal of incrementalism: it does an excellent job of depicting how government operates, but many are uneasy with the mirror it holds up to reality. We believe that incrementalism is not just the best description of the way American government actually works—it is also a source of strength and value.

For his part, Lindblom found the tendency of critics to associate incrementalism with the status quo puzzling. As he noted in a 1979 article entitled "Still Muddling, Not Yet Through," incremental reform is not inherently a "tactic of conservatism":

> A fast-moving sequence of small changes can more speedily accomplish a dramatic alteration from the status quo than can an only infrequent major policy change. . . . Incremental steps can be made quickly because they are only incremental. They do not rock the boat, do not stir up the great antagonisms and paralyzing schisms as do proposals for more drastic change.[31]

A similar analysis has been made by political scientist Martha Derthick, whose analysis of the long gestation of Social Security we will review in Chapter 4. "If analysts would look at the politics of minor increments," she wrote, "they would see in the accretion of them substantial change—even radical change . . . the possibilities of repeated small enlargements are practically endless."[32]

While a proponent of incrementalism, Wildavsky acknowledged that when the underlying conditions that promote incrementalism are no longer present (such as shared agreement about basic norms and relatively stable relationships between institutional partners), it can give way to non-incremental outcomes, or what he called "shift points."[33] To Wildavsky, this was a cause for concern, not celebration: he believed that the loosening of constraints would lead to undesirable results, such as an explosion in the size of governmental debt.

As Wildavsky suggests, incrementalism is normally the way the world works—except for when it isn't. The world trundles along, until suddenly it doesn't. Ernest Hemingway, in *The Sun Also Rises*, offers a pithy description of how a character went bankrupt: "Gradually, then suddenly." This kernel of wisdom has endured for a reason. According to writer Chuck Klosterman, "For almost a century, this insight has been referenced so often that it has become its own kind of cliché, in part because it applies to almost everything. Ernest Hemingway's description of change is the way most things change."[34]

Extreme circumstances—war, famine, depression, etc.—often necessitate extreme solutions. The problem is that in the American marketplace of ideas, every interest group is always claiming a state of emergency in an effort to win support for their pet program or cause, a theme that we will return to in Chapter 8. This creates a "boy who cried wolf" dynamic. The late economist Paul Samuelson captured this phenomenon when he joked that the stock market had predicted nine of the last five recessions. In truth, discerning true crises from rhetorical emergencies is usually only possible after the fact.

Like Lindblom, we believe that incrementalism is not the enemy of change. To the contrary, we think that those who are prepared to recognize the reality of how government actually functions are the most likely to achieve their policy goals.

By design, the structure of the American government makes radical change difficult to accomplish. But this is far from the only obstacle that stands in the way of those who seek to remake our society. Changing laws and winning congressional debates is one thing. What happens on the ground is quite another. Many big ideas are defeated by the challenges of implementation. Those who fail to win over the hearts and minds of frontline government workers will come face to face with the practitioner veto.

2

The Practitioner Veto

"Nobody disobeys my orders," declared President Donald Trump with characteristic bluster in April 2019.[1]

As was often the case, Trump's statement was inaccurate. Indeed, the Trump years were filled with stories of Cabinet officials and other high-ranking staffers defying the president's directives. After he left office, Secretary of State Rex Tillerson reported that he often prevented Trump from getting his way: "I'd have to say to him, 'Mr. President, I understand what you want to do, but you can't do it that way. It violates the law. It violates treaty.'"[2]

Not to be outdone, White House counsel Don McGahn declined to fire special counsel Robert Mueller who was investigating potential Russian interference in the 2016 election. The Mueller report was something of an obsession for Trump, who sought to undermine the investigation in myriad ways. In his final report, Mueller took note of this interference, writing: "The president's efforts to influence the investigation were mostly unsuccessful, but that is largely because the persons who surrounded the president declined to carry out orders or accede to his requests."[3]

But it wasn't just upper-echelon officials that disobeyed President Trump. Throughout the federal government, there were acts of resistance—some minor and symbolic, others more meaningful—by workers at all levels of the hierarchy. With the help of their unions, workers at the Environmental Protection Agency launched a campaign to "Save the EPA" from budget cuts and other policies that they didn't like. Media leaks sprung up in multiple agencies, as staffers fed gossip and internal documents to reporters eager to document the chaos within the Trump administration. Interior Secretary Ryan Zinke claimed that nearly one third of his staff were disloyal and bemoaned the reality that "There's too many ways in the present process for someone who doesn't want to get (a regulatory action) done to put it in a holding pattern."[4]

The *Washington Post* published an op-ed entitled "Staying True to Yourself in the Age of Trump: A How-to Guide for Federal Employees," arguing for "bureaucratic resistance from below."[5] In a similar essay, former State Department official Laura Rosenberg offered this advice to civil and foreign service workers:

> In many ways, you are the last line of defense against illegal, unethical, or reckless actions. . . . History has shown us that implementation of such policies depends on a compliant bureaucracy of obedient individuals who look the other way and do as they are told. Do what bureaucracy does well: slow-roll, obstruct, and constrain. Resist. Refuse to implement anything illegal, unethical, or unconstitutional.[6]

Infuriated that getting his way was harder than he had anticipated, Trump referred to this internal resistance by a nefarious shorthand: the "deep state." Trump would end up blaming many of the failures of his administration on what he perceived to be a permanent, secret government staffed by antagonistic bureaucrats bent on undermining his agenda.

While Trump's extraordinary behavior did prompt an unusual amount of defiance from government workers, the truth is that internal resistance is a regular feature of governance in the United States. According to David Rohde, the author of *In Deep: The FBI, the CIA, and the Truth about America's "Deep State"*:

> Every president has expressed frustration with Washington when they came into office. Reagan complained about the State Department not wanting to fight communism as aggressively as he did. Barack Obama feared that Pentagon officials were leaking possible numbers for a troop

increase in Afghanistan as a way to box him in and force him to send more troops than he wanted to Afghanistan. It's the way it's always been.[7]

What Rohde is describing here is one of the central realities of life in government and one of the principal brakes on systemic change in the United States: the reality that it is all but impossible to govern without the consent of the governed, in this case the rank and file within any government agency. When government workers withhold this consent, they are exercising what we call the practitioner veto.

Street-Level Bureaucrats

Michael Lipsky wasn't thinking about resisting errant presidents when he wrote *Street-Level Bureaucracy* in 1980.

Lipsky, a professor of political science who later served as a program officer at the Ford Foundation, was more concerned with the urban conflicts that roiled the United States in the 1960s and 1970s. His focus was on the work of frontline government officials—"teachers, police officers and other law enforcement personnel, social workers, judges, public lawyers and other court officials, health workers, and many other public officials who grant access to government programs and provide services within them."[8] He was particularly interested in how these officials served, or failed to serve, the interests of poor people and minority groups.

One of Lipsky's key insights was that the workers he identified as "street-level bureaucrats" are not mindless drones who automatically do the bidding of their superiors. Rather, they are individual actors who are more than capable of independent action.

As Lipsky understood, state and local government agencies tend to be challenging environments within which to work. The facilities are often dilapidated, and the technology outmoded. The available resources rarely keep pace with the demand for services. And policy directives, even those embedded in legislation, are never foolproof.

Scientist and philosopher Alfred Korzybski issued a famous dictum that is relevant here: "the map is not the territory." Even the best, most detailed maps cannot accurately represent reality. The same is true for laws, rules, regulations, policy guidebooks, and other documents that seek to dictate the behavior of government officials on the ground. Policies that are crystal-clear when they are written in legislative chambers or in downtown office headquarters often don't make sense out in the field, where government workers must handle individual cases, idiosyncratic clients, and unusual fact patterns. Jeffrey Pressman and Aaron Wildavsky (whom we met in the previous chapter as an expert in budgeting) pointedly captured this idea in the subtitle to their classic book *Implementation: How Great Expectations in Washington DC Are Dashed in Oakland; Or Why It's Amazing That Federal Programs Work at All.*

Between the lines, street-level bureaucrats inevitably wield enormous discretion. And they often use this discretion to resist or undermine diktats from above. The practitioner veto can take many different forms—leaks to the media, whistleblower complaints, lawsuits, and more. Often, the practitioner veto is invisible to the naked eye. Street-level bureaucrats know that if they can just drag their feet for long enough, a new set of political leaders will soon come into their agency with a new set of directives replacing the ones that they object to.

Street-level bureaucrats resist direction for all sorts of reasons. Sometimes their motives are high-minded, as in the case of the federal officials who thought that Trump was violating the rule of law. And sometimes they are simply matters of personal preference, like a desire to move through their daily routine with a minimum of hassle or to ensure that they leave work promptly at 5 P.M.

In *Bureaucracy*, his book about how government agencies work, political scientist James Q. Wilson made the point as follows: "When bureaucrats are free to choose a course of action their choices will reflect the full array of incentives operating on them: some will reflect the need to manage workload; others will reflect the expectations of workplace peers and professional colleagues elsewhere; still others may reflect their own convictions."⁹ Wilson also warns of the dangers of over-regulation, arguing that an over-regulated government work-force tends to be a demoralized workforce. This makes intuitive sense: very few people like to go to work feeling that they are distrusted or that they are being deprived of meaningful autonomy.

Whether the practitioner veto is a force for good or for evil de-pends upon your perspective. Progressive activists might be inclined to applaud the example of government workers rejecting orders from President Trump. They might be less favorably inclined toward what is happening within the Los Angeles District Attorney's Office at the moment of this writing.

George Gascón ran for district attorney in 2020 on a progressive platform. He wasted little time putting his ideas into practice. In short order after his victory, Gascón announced a sweeping set of policy changes, promising (among other things) to end cash bail, to stop seeking the death penalty, and to prevent his attorneys from trying juveniles as adults. Perhaps most controversially, Gascón prohibited his prosecutors from seeking various kinds of sentencing enhancements that traditionally have been used to extend prison sentences for de-fendants suspected of being gang members.

Almost immediately, many of the prosecutors in Los Angeles re-volted. The Association of Deputy District Attorneys, the union that represents Gascón's prosecutors, sued, arguing that Gascón had vio-lated state law.

As with the Trump resisters, Gascón's adversaries portrayed them-selves as defending the rule of law: "You can't just use the law to im-plement your personal worldview of what society should look like," Deputy District Attorney Eric Siddall said. "The idea of one man coming in and saying, 'You all are wrong, and this is what the law should be,' is kind of counter to what our entire American system of justice is all about. It's the antithesis of the rule of law."¹⁰

Remarkably, the California District Attorneys Association, the group that represents California's fifty-eight elected district attorneys, publicly backed the challenge to Gascón. Some opponents even attempted to launch a recall campaign to oust Gascón. Though this effort ultimately failed, the battle of Los Angeles is still raging as we write this, thanks in no small part to significant increases in violent crime, which have only helped to fuel the anger of Gascón's opponents. A similar phenomenon is also taking place in San Francisco and several other cities that have elected progressive prosecutors seeking controversial changes in their local justice systems.

What is happening in these cities is newsworthy in part because it is so unusual. To be sure, most government officials follow most directives, most of the time. Nonetheless, no one is immune to the practitioner veto. Signs of the practitioner veto can be found all around us: in the police officers currently taking early retirement in the wake of new accountability reforms, in the teachers protesting restrictions on teaching critical race theory, and in the 1,200 (!) Rikers Island correctional officers who called in sick on a single day in May 2021.

The practitioner veto calls us to pay attention to the thoughts, feelings, and concerns of government workers. The goal of most reformers, no matter what their ideological coloring, is usually to improve circumstances on the ground, where government intersects with citizens. And this simply can't happen without the active engagement of the people actually charged with doing the work in the field.

Unfortunately, loud voices on both ends of the political spectrum often communicate contempt for government workers. This is particularly true on the right. In the forty years since Ronald Reagan uttered his famous line, "Government is not the solution to our problem, government is the problem," Republican activists have regularly sought to demonize government workers and stifle government action. Activists on the left engage in a different kind of disparagement, denouncing American government institutions as structurally racist and those who work within them as complicit in a host of sins against the less fortunate.

Many efforts to change government simply ignore practitioners altogether, focusing on questions of politics and policy rather than practice. In general, there are three primary avenues for shaping the work of government. Using education as an example:

1. *Politics*—Should I vote for the Democrats or the Republicans? Which candidate should I support for mayor of my city? Can I figure out how to help elect people that I agree with to the local school board? These are fundamentally political questions.

2. *Policy*—Should students be required to wear masks at school? Will my city support charter schools or not? Should standardized testing be used to raise standards and increase accountability? Should teachers be encouraged to use the 1619 Project's curriculum to teach American history? How will admissions to honors programs or specialized high schools be handled? These are all questions of policy.

3. *Practice*—What is actually happening in my kid's classroom? Is the teacher strict or lenient? What is the atmosphere like? What methods are being used to teach reading and mathematics? Is my child learning? Are his classmates? These are questions of practice.

It is seductive to think that if you can elect the right leaders and craft the right policies, you will also change practice on the ground. This kind of straightforward, linear relationship—whereby politicians establish policies that are then implemented by practitioners—may make sense in theory, but it is often not true in practice. The real world can be very messy.

The Program That Actually Occurs

When asked about boxing strategy, Mike Tyson famously claimed that "Everybody has a plan until they get punched in the mouth." What is true in the ring is also true when it comes to government implementation. According to Joseph Durlak, a professor of clinical psychology who specializes in program evaluation, "The program you think you are doing almost never turns out to be the program that actually occurs."[11] Not as vivid as Tyson perhaps, but the same basic gist.

What both Tyson and Durlak are pointing to is a truth that politicians rarely acknowledge: there is a big difference between articulating an idea in a speech or a concept paper or even a law and making it work in the real world. Knowledge is only useful if it is turned into practice on the ground. Or to put it another way: implementation matters.

"The program that actually occurs" will always be shaped, in ways both subtle and profound, by the humans who are charged with implementing it on the ground. The hands-on experience of street-level bureaucrats informs their approach to any new program or policy. And, in general, this practical knowledge tends to point in the direction of incremental rather than radical change.

In recent years, an entire academic field of study has emerged to gain a better understanding of how implementation actually happens. "Implementation science" seeks to facilitate the integration of research evidence into policy and practice. Recognizing that there is a significant gap between knowledge and action, implementation science is founded on a painful truth: success is never guaranteed and there is no such thing as an idiot-proof idea. Unless significant time, energy, and resources are devoted to effective implementation, new programs and policies are likely to fail.

On the flip side, researchers have documented that high-quality implementation does make a difference. According to the US Department of Health and Human Services:

> In a large-scale review of school-based programs involving over 200 studies and over a quarter of a million youth, the benefits demonstrated by students receiving programs associated with higher quality implementation were compared to those participating in programs that were implemented with poorer quality. The former students showed gains in academic performance that were twice as high as the latter group; furthermore, the students in the better implemented programs also showed

a reduction in emotional distress (e.g., depression and anxiety) that was more than double the reduction shown by the latter group and a reduction in levels of conduct problems that was nearly double that of the latter group. In other words, effective implementation can lead to larger gains for youth . . . it is clearly worthwhile to strive for high quality implementation.[12]

This finding may seem self-evident—do we really need researchers to tell us that good programs perform better than bad ones?—but the implications are enormous. If we hope to make the world a better place, with less injustice and better government services for all, then we need to spend more time worrying about practice. This means listening to practitioners.

The two of us have devoted the bulk of our professional careers to attempting to implement programs effectively. Over the years, we have helped to create and administer alternatives to incarceration, youth development projects, violence prevention initiatives, pretrial diversion programs, and more. Much of this work has been performed in collaboration with various government partners.

For example, one of the projects that we both worked on when we were at the Center for Court Innovation was the spread of "problem-solving courts"—specialized courtrooms that sought to focus the energies of the judiciary on solving the underlying problems of defendants and litigants, such as addiction and mental illness. Some of these projects were more successful than others. One of the biggest differences was simply the quality of the judge involved in any given program. The best problem-solving courts tended to have great judges who were good listeners, willing collaborators, and effective communicators from the bench.

In our previous book, *Trial & Error in Criminal Justice Reform: Learning from Failure*, we attempted to distill some of the lessons from our experience. We won't rehash those lessons here, except to say that our experience echoes many of the findings from the research literature. Good implementation is harder than you think. While there are, of course, isolated cases of incompetence and corruption, new initiatives tend to flop for more banal reasons, including running out of money, choosing the wrong staff, and failing to manage inter-agency partnerships effectively. Things can go wrong even for competent, well-intentioned people.

At the heart of effective implementation is a paradox: fidelity and adaptation are both essential. Fidelity means paying close attention to replicating the key elements of any successful intervention, with a particular focus on dosage. If a clinical trial of a given drug shows evidence of success when 10mg was administered, health care professionals need to follow this example. The same idea holds true even when what is being delivered is a reading intervention or a financial literacy program instead of a pharmaceutical fix.

On the other hand, just because a program has worked in one setting doesn't mean it will work everywhere. The local context is always unique. As Billy Bragg has sung: "You can borrow ideas, but you can't borrow situations." Inevitably, new ideas and new programs must be tailored to the idiosyncratic needs and values of particular places and populations. Practitioners must be allowed the freedom to embroider, altering programs and policies at the margins to suit local circumstances, to respond to emerging challenges, and to incorporate new information.

Scale is the rock upon which many encouraging policies and programs have foundered. According to Lisbeth Schorr and Frank Farrow of the Center for the Study of Social Policy,

> The history of replication and scale-up efforts is discouraging. . . . The ascendant belief in the 1960s and 1970s was that successful programs carried the seeds of their own replication. Foundations hoped that when they funded a pilot that worked, it would be picked up by others and supported with public funds and reformed policies. By the end of the 1980s, it became clear that successful programs were dying when the demonstration funds ran out at much the same rate as those that didn't work. Furthermore, when successful programs have been implemented away from their places of origin and taken to scale, they have at best modest results. In his overview of the scale-up scene, Robert Granger [of the William T. Grant Foundation]

concludes that "Despite the research community's ability to identify promising programs, there is almost no evidence that it is possible to take such programs to scale in a way that maintains their effectiveness."[13]

One of the things that has recently hampered the process of solving social problems is that policymakers and researchers have tended to take a restrictive view of what constitutes knowledge.[14] In our experience, one of the most important, and overlooked, sources of knowledge is the wisdom generated by experienced practitioners in the field. A good teacher can tell you a lot about what works in the classroom and what doesn't. The same is true for probation officers, case workers, public housing managers . . . the list goes on.[15]

Put simply, it is difficult to do implementation right without the active involvement of street-level bureaucrats. Unfortunately, the constraints and incentives of American politics often work against this. Engaging with practitioners to understand the problems they face and to solicit their input on possible solutions is not something that can happen overnight—it takes time and effort. It's no wonder that Donald Trump couldn't avoid the practitioner veto; nothing in his history or his character suggests that he has the necessary patience or ability to listen.

One of the principal things that we would learn if we were really interested in listening to practitioners is how important good practitioners are to the success of any endeavor. In a field review entitled "Program Implementation: What Do We Know?," researchers for the organization Child Trends talked to practitioners about what made programs for children successful. According to the report, "When leaders in the field were asked to identify the single most important ingredient for program quality, the overwhelming response was program staff, indicating that they need to be well trained, well compensated and able to foster youth leadership."[16]

This may once again sound obvious and perhaps even self-serving—of course program staff think that they are important! Who doesn't? But it is worth noting that many efforts to solve social problems through government action are in fact focused on other things.

As James Q. Wilson has argued, "the American political system is biased toward solving bureaucratic problems by issuing rules."[17] There are often good reasons for issuing rules, of course—they can effectively establish minimum standards and help protect Americans from the abuses of arbitrary authority. But issuing rules cannot create excellent performance within government agencies. If we truly want our government to work better, we need to make a deeper investment in those who actually deliver government services. This includes rethinking how they are paid and trained.

In recent years, the school system in Washington, DC, historically one of the country's worst, has attempted to do just that. The DC public schools instituted a set of reforms that included a greater emphasis on standardized tests as an evaluation metric and higher pay (including performance bonuses) for DC teachers. The reforms have been controversial, but the results indicate that Washington has succeeded in improving teacher retention among those teachers rated as "effective" and "highly effective." Just as important, the new system in DC has led to the firing of many of the teachers that were rated "ineffective." Reviewing the research, blogger Matt Yglesias reported that when low-rated teachers in DC leave, student achievement improves.[18] The DC experience would seem to suggest that school systems should be doing all that they can to attract, reward, and retain good teachers.

Vision Without Execution Is Hallucination

In his unfinished novel *The Pale King*, David Foster Wallace expressed a sentiment that is common among many, if not most, Americans: a hatred of bureaucracies. "I hated and feared them," he writes,

> and basically regarded them as large, grinding, impersonal machines—
> that is, they seemed rigidly literal and rule-bound the same way

machines are, and just about as dumb. . . . My primary association with the word *bureaucracy* was an image of someone expressionless behind a counter, not listening to any of my questions or explanations of circumstance or misunderstanding but merely referring to some manual of impersonal regulations as he stamped my form with a number that meant I was in for some further kind of tedious, frustrating hassle or expense.[19]

Skepticism about government is part of the American DNA—one of the explicit goals of the Constitution is to limit the powers of government. The two of us are not immune to this feeling. Indeed, one of the motivating forces in our careers has been an instinctive loathing of bureaucracy and a desire for freedom from "large, grinding, impersonal machines."

Given all of this, it may seem counterintuitive that we suggest giving greater voice to those who work within the machinery of American government. But our experience suggests that it is difficult, if not impossible, to change any system without involving the people that actually operate those systems. Thomas Edison said it best: "Vision without execution is hallucination."

To be clear, our argument here is not that the street-level bureaucrats are always right—indeed, it is sometimes their behavior that is most in need of reform. Rather, our argument is that no institutional reform can truly succeed unless it wins the hearts and minds of government practitioners, and that won't happen if they feel that they have not been part of the change process. Progressives should take special note of this reality, since they typically have the most ambitious plans for government.

Anyone with ambitions for expanding the work of government would be well advised to read *The Cost of Good Intentions*, Charles Morris's analysis of what went wrong during New York City mayor John Lindsay's administration in the late 1960s and early 1970s. This was a political moment in which government was being encouraged to do more on behalf of the less fortunate. Morris had an insider's perspective on what happened next—he worked at high levels within

New York City government, including directing the city's welfare and Medicaid programs.

Morris is largely sympathetic to the goals of the Lindsay adminis-tration, which sought to fundamentally reorient government in New York City toward fighting poverty and achieving racial justice. But he is withering in his assessment of its impacts. He concludes:

> The soaring rhetoric of [the Lindsay administration] did not lend itself to easy translation into day-to-day measuring rods of performance and seems to have generated only confusion and hostility among front-line workers. . . . The entire battalion of city agencies—parks, welfare, police, housing, the new anti-poverty programs, hospitals, even sanitation—were to be part of a massive effort at uplift, a final breaking-through of the barriers of oppression and discrimination that prolonged the abject misery of blacks and Hispanics and imposed such heavy costs upon the city. It was a splendid vision, but one that was seriously flawed and, from a management perspective, positively damaging. . . . The sudden call to lofty achievement was, for most agencies, simply muddling. . . . It was never possible to tell—at least on any scale that mattered—whether any of the social intervention programs made a difference . . . the pro-grams had a strong tendency to emphasize symbol over content, to value structure and participation over program results.[20]

In Chapter 7, we will take a deep dive into several Great Society pro-grams and come to a similar conclusion to Morris's: that the reach of these initiatives exceeded their grasp and that more time should have been spent wrestling with the pragmatic details of program implementation.

We wish we could report that today's government reformers have absorbed the lessons of the 1960s and 1970s. But that is not the case. Some lessons have to be learned anew by each generation.

One recent example of this dynamic is the effort by then-Newark mayor Cory Booker and New Jersey governor Chris Christie to com-pletely overhaul the Newark school system with the help of funding from Facebook's Mark Zuckerberg. In her book *The Prize: Who's in Charge of America's Schools?*, journalist Dale Russakoff documents how this systemic change initiative was launched with great fanfare—and then quickly went sideways: "Booker, Christie, and Zuckerberg set out to create a national 'proof point' in Newark. There was less focus on Newark as its own complex ecosystem that reformers needed to understand before trying to save it. Two hundred million dollars and almost five years later, there was at least as much rancor as reform."[21] Russakoff's final judgment was simple: "education reform is too important to be left to reformers alone."

They may be writing about different initiatives taking place in different eras, but Russakoff and Morris are essentially describing the same basic problem: the "policy-implementation gap."[22] The only way to avoid this gap is to ensure that politics and practice are not separate worlds that never intersect. We need practitioners to have a voice in formulating policy. And we need policymakers to have a better grasp on what actually happens at the ground level. Without these things, we are doomed to repeat the failures of the past, ad infinitum.

Ultimately, policymaking comes down to implementation. The lofty rhetoric of speeches and sound bites must be translated into action on the ground. And because the people who are doing the implementing on the ground tend to be incrementalists, this means that policy change will often be incremental, no matter what elected officials and top-down strategists say.

But even if you can get frontline practitioners to buy into a change agenda, there is a more fundamental problem: there is little evidence that the majority of the American public is interested in big change in the first place.

3

What the Public Wants

For a few weeks in 2020, reporter Lee Fang of *The Intercept* found himself in the eye of a social media hurricane. It started, as such controversies often do these days, with a single tweet.

On June 3, 2020, Fang tweeted out a short man-on-the-street video interview that he had conducted, along with this text: "Asked everyone I spoke with today if there was anything they wanted to get off their chest about the movement. Max from Oakland, a supporter of BLM, had a measured critique he wanted to share." During the course of the two-minute clip, Max (who identifies as African American) says this:

> I always question, why does a Black life matter only when a White man takes it? . . . Like, if a White man takes my life tonight, it's going to be national news, but if a Black man takes my life, it might not even be spoken of. . . . It's stuff just like that that I just want in the mix.[1]

At the time that Fang's conversation with Max took place, the entire country seemed to be in turmoil. George Floyd had died at the knees of Derek Chauvin in Minneapolis the previous week. Massive protests against police violence and racism were underway in dozens of cities (accompanied, in some places, by rioting and looting). Senator Tom Cotton's infamous op-ed in the *New York Times* urging the federal government to respond to street unrest was published on the same day as Fang's tweet. The Covid-19 pandemic was still raging. And the 2020 presidential race was starting to heat up. The political atmosphere was, to say the least, febrile.

Even so, the reaction to Fang's tweet was surprising. The problems for Fang started when one of his colleagues at *The Intercept*, a reporter named Akela Lacy, wrote on Twitter: "Tired of being made to deal continually with my co-worker @lhfang continuing to push black on black crime narratives after being repeatedly asked not to. This isn't about me and him, it's about institutional racism and using free speech to couch anti-blackness. I am so fucking tired." She followed with, "Stop being racist Lee."[2]

Lacy's tweets were liked and retweeted hundreds, then thousands, then tens of thousands of times. According to Jonathan Chait of *New York* magazine, "A journalist friend of Fang's told me he felt his career was in jeopardy, having been tried and convicted in a court of his peers. He was losing sleep for days and unsure how to respond. 'All of us were trying to protect his job and clear his name and also not bow to a mob informed by an attitude that views that you disagree with are tantamount to workplace harassment.'"[3]

Fang ended up issuing the requisite public apology two days later, writing:

> When I posted a video by a young black man whom I interviewed, Max, at a Black Lives Matter protest against police violence in the Bay Area, some people, including people I deeply respect, took this as a suggestion that I intended to feed a "black-on-black crime" trope in order to dismiss concerns about police violence. I know very well that there are cynical actors, often racists themselves, who weaponize such tropes, retorting "All Lives Matter" when their true purpose is merely to reject the idea that black people's lives do. I am not one of those people. . . . The United States is an extraordinarily violent country and I believe that the recent scenes of police violence inflicted on protestors nationally are a reflection of that. My concern for the victims of violence, including friends and people I grew up with, is not just genuine but deeply personal. It grieves me to think that people have the opposite impression, or that they believe I would say anything to undermine the fight against structural racism in this country.[4]

What happened to Lee Fang is, first and foremost, a story of one journalist's individual misfortune. But it is also the story of the pernicious effects of social media and the misleading signals it sends about public opinion. It would be easy to come away from Lee Fang's personal and professional crisis thinking that the views he broadcast were heretical or, at the very least, well outside of the American mainstream. The truth is very different.

Conflict Entrepreneurs

The world has always been full of conflict entrepreneurs—people who actively seek to provoke and heighten disagreement. The internet has only amplified their reach and their influence. The incentives of the contemporary media industry, and social media platforms like Twitter and Facebook, reward those who spark the most engagement. And few things are more engaging than outrage.

Conflict entrepreneurs feed on outrage. Indeed, their professional success often depends upon it. Pundits like Nikole Hannah-Jones, Glenn Beck, Glenn Greenwald, and Christopher Rufo have become minor celebrities thanks to their capacity for provocation. Politicians like Ted Cruz and Alexandria Ocasio-Cortez revel in inflammatory rhetoric and ratcheting up the stakes. Media outlets like Fox News and MSNBC have been able to fashion successful business models out of political conflict.

And then there is the greatest conflict entrepreneur of them all: Donald Trump. No figure in recent memory has provoked more extreme reactions than the former president. Trump is a living, breathing litmus test who exists to elicit only two reactions: for or against. As president, Trump dramatically accelerated hyper-partisanship. According to Gallup, 82 percentage points separated Republicans' (89 percent) and Democrats' (7 percent) job approval ratings of President Trump during his third year in office. This was the largest party gap in presidential approval that Gallup had ever measured. Second place went to Trump's second year in office, when there was a 79-point party gap.[5]

In recent years, Trump and other conflict entrepreneurs have helped to foster an atmosphere of what journalist Amanda Ripley calls "high conflict." According to Ripley,

> Conflict can be a force for good, pushing us to challenge each other and defend ourselves and do better. But sometimes, it escalates into something else, something called *high conflict*. High conflict is what happens when discord distills into a good-versus-evil kind of feud, the kind with an *us* and a *them*. High conflict acts like a spell, bewitching us without our realizing what is happening. The brain behaves differently. People feel increasingly certain of their own superiority and, at the same time, more and more mystified by the other side. Both sides feel the same emotions, though they never discuss it with each other.[6]

By many measures, political polarization in the United States has increased in recent years. For example, a 2017 report by the Pew Research Center documented that divisions between Republicans and Democrats on a host of issues, including race, immigration, and aid to the needy, have widened considerably since 1994.[7] In 1994, Democrats and Republicans were about equally likely to agree with the statement that "immigrants strengthen the country with their hard work and talents"—32 percent of Democrats agreed with that statement, compared to 30 percent of Republicans. By 2017, the gap had become a gulf—84 percent of Democrats agreed, compared to 42 percent of Republicans.

In another poll, Pew found that the overall share of Americans who express consistently conservative or consistently liberal opinions had doubled during the period 1994–2014, from 10 percent to 21 percent. The researchers concluded, "Partisan animosity has increased substantially. . . . In each party, the share with a highly negative view of the opposing party has more than doubled since 1994. Most of these intense partisans believe the opposing party's policies 'are so misguided that they threaten the nation's well-being.'"[8]

Tufts University professor Eitan Hersh, the author of *Politics Is for Power*, blames some of this polarization on "political hobbyists."

Hersh believes that real politics is about "the methodical pursuit of power to influence how the government operates." In contrast, political hobbyists are more likely to spend their time consuming the news than volunteering in political organizations. Political hobbyists treat politics like a parlor game, an opportunity to debate abstract issues. "What they are doing is no closer to engaging in politics than watching SportsCenter is to playing football," says Hersh.[9]

Jeff Plaut is a partner at Global Strategy Group, a consulting firm that does polling for Democratic candidates. According to Plaut, "When we used to ask the question 'Are things going in the right direction or off on the wrong track?,' voters' answers used to largely reflect their personal economic situation. Now, it reflects their views of their political leaders and whether they like the Democratic or Republican leader in office."[10]

What Plaut is talking about here is the concept of "affective polarization"—the tendency to automatically dislike or distrust ideas associated with your partisan opponents. There are some indications that affective polarization is intensifying in the United States, warping not only our politics but even seemingly non-political topics like Covid-19 vaccinations and perceptions of the weather (with Democrats much more likely to report noticing extreme weather events than Republicans).[11]

The role that social media has played in all of this is significant. A 2014 study involving more than 600,000 Facebook users found that Facebook's News Feed was a locus of social contagion, transferring emotional states from one user to another: "When positive expressions (in the News Feed) were reduced, people produced fewer positive posts and more negative posts; when negative expressions were reduced, the opposite pattern occurred. These results indicate that emotions expressed by others on Facebook influence our own emotions, constituting experimental evidence for massive-scale contagion via social networks."[12]

In a 2021 study that looked at 12.7 million tweets from 7,331 Twitter users, researchers from Yale University found that the social media platform incentivized users to express more outrage over time—users who received more likes and retweets when they expressed outrage in a tweet were more likely to express outrage in later posts. "Our data show that social media platforms do not merely reflect what is happening in society," said Molly Crockett, one of the authors of the study. "Platforms create incentives that change how users react to political events over time."[13]

Theorist Marshall McLuhan coined the expression "the medium is the message" in 1964. In doing so, McLuhan calls us to pay attention not just to content but to the vehicles through which content is communicated. He argues that the medium itself helps determine what kind of ideas get expressed and how they are received.

We are still in the early days of social media, but, as McLuhan would have predicted, it already seems to be affecting behavior in ways both subtle and seismic. Platforms like Facebook and Twitter tend to promote brevity, urgency, and virality. All of these dynamics play into the hands of conflict entrepreneurs, who feed off of division. According to writer Wesley Yang, "It is said that the first movie audiences ran in terror from the image of an approaching train, believing it to be real. Similarly, the first people and institutions exposed to social media mobs groveled at the sight of what appeared to be an overwhelming consensus."[14]

Many critics, observing the latest online controversy, will roll their eyes and dutifully remind us that "Twitter is not real life." This is, of course, true—polling suggests that only one in five Americans use Twitter. However, it doesn't account for the fact that Twitter is increasingly influencing political debates and molding political personalities offline as well as on. It will be decades before we fully understand the impacts of social media on our public discourse—and figure out ways to counteract its pernicious influence.

Public Judgment

Daniel Yankelovich, who died in 2017, was known as the dean of public opinion research. The founder of one of the largest market research companies in the United States, Yankelovich believed that there is a difference between public opinion and what he labeled "public judgment." Yankelovich believed that public opinion changed constantly. It is by its nature superficial and inconsistent. It is raw and reactive, subject to being moved by the latest headlines. It can also be manipulated by small tweaks in how questions are worded.

Public judgment, however, is something different. Unlike public opinion, it is more stable. It also takes time to emerge—it represents beliefs that the majority of the public has come to accept as true after a process of deliberation. (There are echoes here of James Madison's "seasoned majority" formulation that we discussed in Chapter 1.) According to Yankelovich, public judgments are not just more thoughtful than public opinions, they also are more likely to focus on moral values and ethical concerns.

Yankelovich's formulation helps us to make sense of the reality that the public is capable of both great stupidity and great insight. In the heat of the moment, we are susceptible to demagoguery and calls for mob justice. But collectively we also possess common-sense wisdom.

In a book entitled *Toward Wiser Public Judgment*, Yankelovich and his coauthor Will Friedman argue that, when public judgment emerges, the public often has insights that elude elite experts. Among other things, they argue that the general public brings to the table "a down-to-earth practicality, a non-ideological pragmatic focus, and a strong insistence on the values that hold our society together."[15]

It is worth noting that Yankelovich and Friedman contrast public judgment with expert opinion. There is often a significant gap between elite views and the views of the general public. This is something that Christopher Lasch put his finger on in his influential 1995 book *The Revolt of the Elites and the Betrayal of Democracy*, where he writes that "the thinking classes have seceded not just from the common world around them but from reality itself."[16] This disconnect has important political implications: as Lasch ruefully notes, the political instincts of the masses are "demonstrably more conservative than those of their self-appointed spokesmen and would-be liberators."[17] One shudders to imagine what Lasch might have made of Twitter, which offers moment-to-moment reminders of the enormous divide between the general public and the "thinking classes."[18]

If you go beyond Twitter, however, it is possible to find indications that Americans are not as divided as they often appear these days. For example, according to Gallup, Americans' opinions about capitalism have remained steady over the past decade, with roughly six out of ten respondents viewing capitalism positively. (Both Democrats and Republicans rated capitalism positively.) Survey respondents were even more favorably inclined toward "free enterprise," with 87 percent evaluating that term positively. In contrast, socialism was viewed negatively by 57 percent of respondents.[19]

While Gallup documented small increases from 2010 to 2019 in the number of respondents who said that they supported a more activist government, when pollsters asked whether people would be willing to pay additional taxes in order to underwrite increased government activity, support plummeted—only 25 percent agreed that there should be both increased government services and increased taxes. Indeed, only 45 percent of Democrats were in favor of the combination of increased services and taxes. (The percentage of Americans who say that their taxes are too low has never risen above 4 percent in more than sixty years of Gallup polling.)[20]

Reviewing these results, Gallup senior scientist Frank Newport came to a stark conclusion: "There is no evidence of strong majority support for government to become more heavily involved in Americans' lives in an effort to solve problems and make things better for the nation's citizens . . . there has been no coming to public judgment on the issue of government's role in our society. There is no public consensus on whether the government should expand to take on more roles in solving societal problems (and by necessity raise more money through taxes to do so) or shrink its involvement."[21]

Not all of the survey research findings are bad for lefties. As Matt Grossman, the director of the Institute for Public Policy and Social Research at Michigan State, has argued, "Americans have long agreed with Republicans in broad symbolic terms while agreeing with Democrats in concrete policy terms."[22]

For instance, after decades of sustained advocacy and consciousness-raising, more than two thirds of Americans approve of gay marriage. A similar percentage of Americans think marijuana use should be legalized. And two out of three agree that human activities are responsible for global warming.[23] On a similar theme, research conducted by Public Agenda, *USA Today*, and Ipsos documented broad support for such policy prescriptions as raising the minimum wage, investing in infrastructure, and creating pathways to citizenship for undocumented immigrants.[24]

Given this general agreement across a range of issues, it should come as little surprise that a survey conducted for the Carr Center for Human Rights and the Institute of Politics at Harvard University found that more than two thirds of Americans agree that they "have more in common with each other than many people think," including 74 percent of Democrats, 78 percent of Republicans, and 66 percent of Independents.[25] "Overall I think Americans want not to be divided as politics are forcing it to be, and that's probably the biggest message of this poll," said John Shattuck of the Carr Center. "Division is not what most Americans are seeking."[26]

A 2018 YouGov/More in Common survey of 8,000 Americans entitled *Hidden Tribes: A Study of America's Polarized Landscape* found that America had splintered into seven "tribes" distinguished by distinct values. There were vast differences in beliefs between "progressive activists" on the left and "devoted conservatives" on the right. But, in between these two poles, the researchers identified an "exhausted majority" whose members do not conform to the partisan ideology of either conservatives or progressives. What these people, who comprise the bulk of the American public, share is "a sense of fatigue with our polarized national conversation, a willingness to be flexible in their political viewpoints, and a lack of voice in the national conversation."[27] Sixty-five percent of the exhausted majority indicated that they wanted to see more compromise in politics.

The Single Most Powerful Force in
American Politics

In making the case for a $3.5 trillion federal spending plan in 2021, Senate Majority Leader Chuck Schumer declared, "It is big, bold change—the kind of change America thirsts for."[28] As we have seen, this kind of rhetorical move is not uncommon these days. Many politicians on both sides of the aisle (not to mention pundits, scholars, and activists) are apt to say that the public is hungry for radical change. But the preponderance of evidence suggests that there is no such hunger among the majority of Americans.

New York Times columnist Paul Krugman argues that one of the currents that runs through both political parties is "the persistent delusion that a hidden majority of American voters either supports or can be persuaded to support radical policies, if only the right person were to make the case with sufficient fervor."[29] Former president Barack Obama, speaking to candidates and activists within the Democratic Party in 2019, put it more succinctly: "The average American doesn't think we have to completely tear down the system and remake it."[30]

In recent years, David Shor, a data scientist who works for Democratic clients, has been relentless in trying to hammer this point home to progressive audiences. In a since deleted tweet, he wrote: "The median voter is 50 and has a mortgage. There isn't actually a ton of appetite for radical policy change. This is why there's currently a Democratic governor in Kansas and a Republican governor in Vermont . . . voters strongly punish parties that visibly try to do stuff! I personally want radical policy change! But it's important to try to make radical stuff seem incremental and reasonable rather than doing the exact opposite."[31] In a 2021 interview, Shor went further, saying, "The biggest single analytical mistake I see a lot of my friends on the Left make is that a lot of people think voters want bold policy change and actually status quo bias and the desire to *not* see policy change is probably the single most powerful force in American politics."[32]

Inspired by Shor's analysis, we went looking to see if there was any survey data to support our argument that the American public is not in a revolutionary mood. We found lots of polls that kind of/sort of touched on this question, but nothing that hit the nail on the head. (It may be out there, of course. We just didn't find it.)

Sensing a gap in knowledge, we reached out to the friendly pollsters at YouGov and asked them to help us. After some back and forth, they agreed to perform a survey with a representative sample of more than 1,000 registered voters. Respondents were asked the following:

Which of the following statements best describes how you would like American government to work:

- *I would generally prefer that government make big, bold changes quickly*
- *I would generally prefer that government make small, gradual changes over time*
- *I would generally prefer that government not change things.*

The results will come as little surprise to anyone who has read this far. Only 34 percent of the respondents said that they would prefer bold change. Forty-five percent favored incrementalism, and 21 percent wanted government not to change things.

One of the more striking results of our survey was the consistency of views about gradualism: Democrats, Republicans, and Independents all approved of incrementalism at roughly the same rate. In all three groups, between 44 and 46 percent of respondents favored gradual change. The same consistency of views about gradualism held true by gender (47 percent of men and 44 percent of women supported the gradual approach), education, and family income. In each case, support for gradualism ranged from 40 to 51 percent, no matter how you cut the data.

As might be expected, there was a pronounced gap in levels of support for bold change between Democrats and Republicans—49 percent of Democrats agreed with the statement that government should make bold change, as opposed to 18 percent of Republicans and 30 percent of Independents. (Still, it is worth noting that, even among Democrats, the majority did *not* favor bold change.)[33] Support for bold change increased as you moved up the education ladder: 43 percent of respondents with postgraduate education favored bold change, as opposed to only 25 percent of individuals with a high school degree or less (35 percent of college graduates favored bold change).

Black respondents (52 percent) viewed the idea of bold change much more favorably than White respondents (31 percent). White respondents were slightly more likely to support gradual change (45 percent) than Black respondents (39 percent).

But the most significant differences emerged when the data were broken down by ideology. Across over sixty demographic and population categories, no group of survey respondents was less supportive of gradual change and more supportive of bold change than those who self-identify as "very liberal." Only 23 percent of very liberal respondents said they favored gradual change, versus 72 percent who supported bold change. Support for gradualism was highest among those who self-identify as moderates (53 percent) and polled at between 43 and 46 percent among liberals, conservatives, and very conservative respondents.

This strong support for bold change among very liberal voters (who comprise about 15 percent of the electorate, according to a 2020 Pew Research Study, matching the proportion in our survey[34]) may help to explain why it is so easy to find calls for bold change on platforms like Twitter, where users tend to skew to the left.[35]

We don't want to overreact to a single poll, even one that we commissioned. Our results are suggestive rather than dispositive. Still, when combined with the other surveys that we have cited, the results tend to strengthen our conviction that there is not a groundswell of public support for systematic change in the United States at the moment, except among the small subset of Americans who identify as progressives.

Defund the Police vs. Blue Lives Matter

And so we return to the case of Lee Fang.

Race and crime have long been vexed topics in the United States—and fertile ground for conflict entrepreneurs. The success of Black Lives Matter has encouraged both counterreaction ("Blue Lives Matter") and overreaction ("Defund the Police"). These banners have been taken up by ideologues and provocateurs who have further inflamed our already heated public discourse.

All of which helps to explain why Fang's seemingly innocuous tweet tripped a wire. Many progressives have identified "black-on-black crime" as a pernicious conservative "trope." They blame the specter of black criminality for the punitive lawmaking, and the subsequent increase in incarceration, that took place across the United States over the past forty years. Anyone who summons this ghost, as Fang did, is immediately suspected of malign, and probably racist, intent.

The Twitter users who mobbed Fang were emblematic of this line of thinking. What they were not emblematic of is the bulk of Americans.

In the days and months since Fang became a target on Twitter, it has become increasingly clear that most Americans care a great deal about violent crime on their streets. According to a 2021 Navigator Research poll, 54 percent of Americans think violent crime is a "major crisis," ranking it above the coronavirus, climate change, inflation, voter suppression, and every other issue of the day. Tellingly, there was almost no difference in perception between Democrats and Republicans—57 percent of Republicans labeled violent crime a major crisis, compared to 52 percent of Democrats.[36]

Despite the efforts of Black Lives Matter and many mainstream media outlets to focus public attention on police brutality, there remains fairly broad support for policing among the American public. According to a 2020 Gallup study, when asked whether they want the police to spend more time, the same amount of time or less time than they currently do in their area, most Black Americans—81 percent— want the police presence either to remain the same or to increase. The numbers were similar for White Americans (88 percent).[37]

Of course, the United States is not a Black and White country. As the 2020 census indicates, the growth in the American population is largely driven by increases among Hispanics and Asian Americans. According to the Gallup study on policing, Hispanics responded simi- larly to White and Black Americans. Asian Americans, however, were slightly more critical of existing patterns of policing, with 28 percent responding that they wanted the police to spend *less* time in their area.[38]

The unpopularity of "Defund the Police" among people of all racial and ethnic backgrounds has been well documented. A *USA Today*/Ipsos poll found that only 22 percent of respondents supported "the movement known as 'defund the police.'" In contrast, seven in ten supported *increasing* police budgets.[39]

In another *USA Today* poll, Detroit residents reported "being much more worried about public safety than about police misconduct. . . . By an overwhelming 9–1 [ratio], they would feel safer with more cops on the street, not fewer." Black residents ranked crime at the top of their list of concerns. Just 3 percent named police reform as their top concern.[40]

Criminal justice is not the only arena where it is possible to argue that the elites who run nonprofits, craft legislation, and write op-eds have gotten out of touch with public sentiment. But so what? Why does it matter if the thinking classes in this country (including not just those who work in politics but also the mainstream media, academia, philanthropy, etc.) are advancing a set of ideas that are not supported by the bulk of the American public?

The answer is that the public's voice cannot be ignored forever. Like the return of the repressed, public opinion will eventually make itself felt. Sometimes this will be through the formal democratic process, as elected officials who are associated with unpopular ideas suffer defeat at the ballot box. Sometimes, as we have seen in Chapter 2, this will take the form of the practitioner veto, as teachers or social workers or other government workers effectively refuse to implement ideas that they find objectionable. And sometimes the revolt of the public will take the form of direct protest, whether online or in the real world.

But the principal reason we must pay attention to public opinion is that it can often lead us toward a set of reforms that might be success-fully implemented without generating enormous backlash. For ex-ample, beneath the Sturm und Drang of the past several years, a fairly broad public consensus seems to be emerging about issues of race, crime, and justice. The polling suggests that Americans care deeply about crime and reject radical policy prescriptions like defunding or abolishing the police. But that does not mean that they are satisfied with the status quo.

According to a Gallup poll, the majority of Americans support reforming the police. Among the reform ideas with broad public support are: requiring officers to have good relations with the com-munity, establishing greater accountability for officer misconduct, preventing officers with a history of abuses from serving, and pro-moting community-based alternatives to policing.[41]

These findings are echoed in a 2020 Public Agenda survey that documented that only 7 percent of respondents wanted law enforce-ment to stay the same. The Public Agenda poll found broad support for reforms such as establishing independent civilian oversight com-mittees, recruiting more Black police officers, requiring de-escalation training, instituting community policing, and creating a public data-base detailing officers who have used excessive force. Beyond po-licing, the survey documented that 76 percent of Americans think that racial bias is a serious problem.[42]

Determining when public judgment emerges is more art than sci-ence. But, when it comes to criminal justice in the United States, a reasonable case can be made that the public has come to endorse a range of incremental reforms that, if implemented, would reduce both racial harms and punitive excess. Various gun control measures, including universal background checks, are supported by large majorities of Americans. According to Gallup, in 1992, 83 percent of Americans said that the justice system was "not tough enough." By 2020, this number had been cut in half, to 41 percent.[43] And an experiment conducted by Public Agenda suggests that when Americans have a chance to learn more about alternative sentencing schemes for nonviolent cases, and to engage in conversation about the topic, they will move away from supporting incarceration as a primary response to offending.[44]

In short, there is a clear path forward for anyone who is interested in advancing criminal justice reform that would be politically popular across a broad swath of the American public. Whether politicians will follow this roadmap—or get distracted by the noise generated by extreme voices on both sides of the political spectrum—will be the challenge of the next several years.

Advancing radical change is hard, particularly in the United States. As we have seen, the public doesn't want it. The very structures of American government are designed to work against it. And practitioners are liable to veto any big ideas that they do not endorse. All of these real-world constraints point in the same direction: toward incrementalism. But what has incrementalism ever achieved? In our next three chapters, we will argue that the incremental approach is actually capable of delivering the kind of significant change that radicals would like to see. You just have to wait for it.

SECTION II

Incrementalism in Action

4

Social Security's Heroic
Incrementalists

In the middle of the Great Depression, two competing approaches to addressing grinding poverty among the elderly competed for political attention. The first approach was radical, easy to understand, and capable of mobilizing one of the largest citizen movements of the twentieth century. The second was slow to develop, internally contradictory, and seemed hopelessly inadequate to the urgency of the moment.

Which path to take? This was the challenge that confronted President Franklin Delano Roosevelt and the band of reformers who sought to improve the lives of American senior citizens in the 1930s. The implications of this decision would reverberate for decades, ultimately affecting millions of Americans.

The New Deal is widely viewed as the pinnacle of progressive lawmaking in the United States. The conventional wisdom is that FDR harnessed the social unrest created by the Great Depression to, almost overnight, launch the New Deal. In so doing, he changed American politics forever.

But what if this understanding is wrong?

For it was the gradual, muddled, and intentionally incremental approach to addressing poverty among the elderly that ultimately prevailed with FDR and his advisors. The result is Social Security, the single largest government program in the United States, costing over

$1 trillion a year, and possibly the most successful anti-poverty initiative ever created. The development and eventual flourishing of Social Security offers some important lessons about the power of incrementalism.

Cautious Reformers

It is hard to find heroes as unlikely as Edwin E. Witte and Arthur J. Altmeyer. Both were born in the late nineteenth century in Wisconsin and came to be identified with the so-called Wisconsin idea of good government. Both were modest and even-tempered. Tellingly, the title of Witte's biography is *Edwin E. Witte: Cautious Reformer*.

Their temperamental humility extended to their beliefs about social change. Witte and Altmeyer were not theoreticians; they believed that practical, real-world experience was more important than abstract reasoning. Their mentor at the University of Wisconsin was the economist John R. Commons, who summed up this philosophy in a 1926 essay about the trade unionist Samuel Gompers. Commons praised Gompers for his habit of "reaching conclusions gradually" through experimentation. "Which is the greater intellect," wrote Commons pointedly, "the brilliant scholar who propounds anything or everything and leads nowhere, or the slow-minded Gompers" who "waits patiently for decades, theorizing and experimenting?"[1]

Social Security would end up being a real-world application of this philosophy. Witte and Altmeyer both had strong ideas about how Social Security should be organized—and even stronger ideas about how it should *not* be organized. They were opponents of what today would be understood as a Universal Basic Income–like program for all older people funded out of general government revenues, which they thought would be politically and practically unworkable. In addition, they feared that a fixed program would foreclose the opportunity to make adjustments and improvements over time.

Today, Social Security pays an average monthly benefit of around $1,500 to 55 million retirees and their dependents. A form of insurance against lost employment income funded through payroll taxes, Social Security represents 23 percent of the entire federal budget, larger than any other federal budget item. It is seen (justly) as the cornerstone of FDR's New Deal legacy.

At the time, however, Social Security was relatively minor compared to other, better known New Deal initiatives.[2] While Social Security was established through legislation in 1935, the first payment wasn't made until January 31, 1940, when the US Treasury issued a $22.54 check to Ida May Fuller of Vermont. Only a small percentage of retirees were even eligible for Social Security benefits until 1950. This left elderly people in a difficult bind, as private pensions weren't a workable alternative: only about 10 percent of industrial workers had employer-provided pension plans, and most of them had been wiped out by the Great Depression anyway.[3]

Until 1950, Social Security was even overshadowed by its twin, the Old Age Assistance Program, or OAA. (When we think of Social Security today, we are thinking of what was originally called the Old-Age and Survivors Insurance Trust Fund, or OASI, to distinguish it from OAA.) OAA was a block grant to states for low-income elderly people that operated more like a traditional welfare program. Its goal, though implementation varied from state to state, was to provide a modest income floor to the elderly unrelated to their own contributions. As late as 1949, OAA supported more than twice as many people as OASI, and average monthly grants were higher ($42 from OAA, as opposed to $25 from OASI).

It took fifteen years—and the successful progression through three so-called founding moments in 1935, 1939, and 1950—for Social Security to emerge as the program we understand it to be today. This was the period of maximum vulnerability for Social Security. At any point in these fifteen years, it could have been derailed or it could have taken on a completely different form. During this period, Witte and Altmeyer worked assiduously to protect Social Security from various threats—Witte as the primary author of the Social Security Act of 1935 and Altmeyer as the program's chief executive from 1937 to 1953.

A Bold and Immediate Rival Solution

One of the biggest threats to Social Security came from an unlikely source: a sixty-seven-year old physician from Long Beach, California named Francis E. Townsend, who mobilized a massive national movement with his vision for a bold and immediate solution to poverty and the Great Depression.

The Townsend movement had humble origins, starting with a letter to the editor of the *Long Beach [Calif.] Press Telegram* on September 30, 1933, in which Townsend proposed giving every American over the age of sixty $150 a month, in exchange for their commitment to immediately retire and spend the money by the end of the month.[4] Townsend would soon increase the offer to $200 a month. Not only would the Townsend plan stimulate the economy, the notion went, but by forcing retirement at age sixty, the plan would create job opportunities for younger people.

The response to the letter was so enthusiastic that Townsend published a follow-up ad to solicit volunteers to promote his ideas, and in January 1934, partnered with his employer—a real estate agent and entrepreneur named Robert Earl Clements—to create a series of "Townsend Clubs" across the country. This was a fertile time for social movements of all kinds—the nation's unemployment rate had reached 25 percent and one-fifth of Americans were forced to survive on paltry direct relief or work relief benefits.

Townsend Clubs eventually enrolled nearly one out of every five Americans over the age of sixty. At its peak, Townsend boasted of a total membership of 3.5 million and 7,000 active clubs,[5] a size that Townsend biographer Edwin Amenta claims was "never reached by any organization in the civil rights or women's movement."[6] By advocating for the interests of elderly individuals, the clubs were a forerunner of the American Association of Retired People, founded in 1958.

Townsend is not an easy person to get a handle on, in part because it's hard to unravel the complicated mix of selfish and public-spirited motives that the Townsend Clubs represented. Townsend himself appeared to be a true believer, but his partner, Clements, who by all accounts was a more effective administrator, approached the enterprise more as a cold-hearted businessman. Thanks to Clements, the Townsend Clubs developed an organizational model that resembled Amway, in which regional (and then state) agents split receipts from the sale of Townsend publications and annual membership fees. These revenues helped support generous salaries for Townsend, Clements, and a small coterie of national leaders.

Townsend later forced Clements out, in part because of criticism that the clubs' true motives were profit, not advocacy. However, as Amenta documents, Townsend's move from figurehead to lead administrator coincided with a disastrous decline in fortune for the clubs. (Amenta likens Townsend to former New York Yankees owner George Steinbrenner, who needed competent administrators to fuel his success.)

Leadership and strategic failures aside, there were evident flaws in the basic concept, which political scientist Martha Derthick dismisses as "preposterous" because it would have cost half the nation's wealth without any plausible funding mechanism. This is not to mention the challenge of enforcing required retirement at age sixty, to say nothing of the wisdom of doing so.[7]

With the benefit of hindsight, Townsend's idea seems doomed from the start. But this was far from clear in the 1930s. Townsend's scheme had several things going for it. Most notable was how immediately the benefits would arrive, in contrast to the Old-Age and Survivors Insurance Trust Fund. Townsend had also become a political force to be reckoned with. He endorsed a number of congressional candidates, and those endorsements carried significant weight in states where there were a lot of Townsend Clubs, particularly in the West and Northwest. (For example, in 1936, Oregon had 415 Townsend Clubs spread out over three congressional districts.)[8] Townsend-endorsed candidates elected to Congress were happy to advocate for the Townsend Plan, and the media attention the movement received helped to further fuel the plan's popularity.

A Contest of Ideas

Witte and Altmeyer recognized the Townsend Plan as a serious threat. In June 1934, they were invited to come to Washington, DC, to serve in key leadership roles on FDR's Committee on Economic Security. Their specific task was to develop a legislative program for the new Congress. Their big idea, as summarized by Altmeyer, was to create a "long-range program through a contributory social insurance system rather than by an increase in general taxation."

The popularity of the Townsend Plan was in some ways a useful foil for Witte and Altmeyer. Luckily for them, in FDR they found a kindred spirit—and someone who was uniquely positioned to resist Townsend's bold notions.

Witte was a fervent opponent of the Townsend plan, believing it to be (in the words of Witte's biographer) "a cruel fraud" that raised false hopes among the poor and the elderly. With an assist from Altmeyer, Witte wrote an important speech that FDR delivered in November 1934 at the National Conference on Economic Security. The speech made it seem as though the president was backing away from pro-posing Social Security legislation because of Townsend. "I do not know whether this is the time for any federal legislation on old age security," FDR said. "Organizations promoting fantastic schemes have aroused hopes that cannot possibly be fulfilled and have greatly in-creased the difficulties of getting sound legislation."

If the idea was to try to lower expectations and send a message to the Townsendites, FDR and his aides overshot their mark. After a bout of bad publicity (and internal unrest), the administration went into damage-control mode. A few days later, New York City mayor Fiorello La Guardia released a letter from FDR assuring him that "undoubtedly" the next Congress would consider old-age pensions.[9]

Despite this misstep, in general Witte and Altmeyer greatly benefited from FDR's political instincts. While not particularly interested in the administrative details, FDR had a keen sense of what was politically tenable. FDR's political genius was to frame Social Security not as a handout to the poor, but as the government equivalent of a private pension plan that was funded through payroll contributions.

This move turned out to be crucial, both in terms of political dynamics and public opinion. The idea was to establish some rough equivalency between the taxes paid into Social Security and the benefits received. This made the program more politically secure because beneficiaries would believe that they had earned the benefits and would be furious if they were threatened. At the same time, tying benefit levels to work would make it seem like less of a handout.

This innovative framing was a clever but arguably risky way to set up a massive benefits program. Originally, OASI was not designed to pay out benefits to a single recipient until 1942, or seven years after it began collecting a 2 percent dedicated payroll tax, divided equally between employees and employers, that was applied to the first $3,000 of earnings. Even then, the maximum benefit provided in the 1935 Act would amount to only $17 per month. Thus, not only did the program itself delay the payment of meager benefits for many years, but those benefits came from a regressive tax—by definition, people with lower income pay a higher tax rate than individuals with higher incomes because of the income cap. (This is still the case: in 2021, Social Security payroll taxes are only applied to wages of $142,800 or less. There is no cap on the Medicare portion of the payroll tax, however.)

The contrast to the Townsend Plan couldn't be more glaring. With Townsend, generous payments of $200 each month for everyone over sixty would start immediately. In comparison, by 1949, even with the more generous benefits introduced in a series of 1939 amendments,

OASI and OAA combined would only pay out an average benefit of $67 monthly.

In a message attached to the successfully passed legislation, President Roosevelt explicitly endorsed the gradualism inherent in the design of the program. "It is overwhelmingly important to avoid," he wrote, "permanently discrediting (Social Security) by attempting to apply it on too ambitious a scale before actual experience has provided guidance for the permanent safe direction of such efforts."[10]

Delayed Gratification

One of the most striking things about Social Security is how fundamental it is in our daily lives. Consider, for example, your Social Security number. If you have one, you probably can recite it from memory.

The original purpose of assigning a Social Security number to each working US citizen and an Employee identification number to employers was to allow the government to track contributions into OASI—without knowing exactly how much money a beneficiary had contributed into the system, it was impossible to pay out benefits accurately.[11] (This level of administrative complexity would not have been necessary under the Townsend Plan.)

Over time, however, Social Security numbers have proven to be so useful as an identifier that they have served a proliferation of purposes: the Social Security Administration website lists twenty-seven "official" governmental uses, including for food stamps, school lunches, student loans, and other federal benefits. Private entities such as banks also regularly request Social Security numbers for identification purposes. (One shudders to imagine the reaction that would ensue if the Biden administration attempted to introduce a universal identifying number today—the cries of "government overreach" and "socialism" would probably be audible from outer space. But the Great Depression was a different time and a different political moment.)

In addition to deferring the payment of OASI benefits, the 1935 Social Security Act delayed implementation of aspects of the Act until January 1, 1937. The Bureau of Internal Revenue (that was what it was called at the time) was in charge of collecting payroll taxes, but it was the Social Security Board and Altmeyer who faced the daunting task of assigning Social Security and Employee identification numbers to tens of millions of workers and hundreds of thousands of employers.

In July 1936, Altmeyer turned to the Postmaster General and the nation's 45,000 post offices to complete the job. By the following year, over thirty million applications had been received by the Social Security Board. In an era before electronic recordkeeping, the Board was inundated with a blizzard of individual workers' pay slips sent in by employers. The solution was to create a decentralized system of data warehouses across the country. By June 1940, Altmeyer could write that "99.2 per cent of the 312 million wage items reported in those years had already been posted to 50 million employee accounts." These records (which included 163 million names) would not be converted from paper to microfilm until 1959.[12]

These kinds of mind-numbing administrative details often get lost in the description of new policy ideas. And we are only hinting at the challenges of establishing a national recordkeeping system—if you're interested in more detail, the Social Security Administration website is happy to help! But it does point to something essential and enduring about Social Security, which is the basic competence of the program's administrators.

Even after the initial authorizing legislation passed in 1935, Social Security faced a series of existential threats. During the 1936 presidential election, Republican candidate Alf Landon denounced Social Security, calling it a "fraud on the working man" and charging that "the saving it forces on our workers is a cruel hoax." The Hearst newspapers ran front page stories denouncing the system, including a cartoon of a man stripped to the waist wearing a chain with a dog tag (presumably containing his Social Security number) with a caption that read "Snooping-Tagging." The Social Security Board responded by distributing 50

million explanatory leaflets that explained the process behind the assign-
ment of Social Security numbers. With the cooperation of labor unions,
these leaflets were given out at factories across the country.

Townsend made a disastrous attempt to use the 1936 presidential
election to expand support for his plan. He endorsed a third-party
candidate while simultaneously urging California club members to
endorse Landon. Townsend thought he could deny any candidate an
Electoral College majority, and later throw the election to whoever
promised to implement the Townsend Plan immediately, a plan that
was foiled when FDR won in a landslide.

The more immediate challenge faced by proponents of Social
Security was the threat that the US Supreme Court would declare
the entire scheme unconstitutional. The Supreme Court had already
struck down the National Recovery Administration and Agricultural
Adjustment Administration (among a number of prominent New
Deal initiatives), and they were scheduled, in 1937, to rule on a case
involving Social Security. This led to one of the more infamous
events in American political history: FDR's unsuccessful court-packing
attempt, followed by the famous "switch in time to save nine"—the
Supreme Court's abrupt reversal in course, which included declaring
Social Security constitutional in 1937.[13]

Social Security had survived several critical challenges, and it was
time to set it on a more secure footing. The issue that consumed
Washington in 1939 was what to do with the large, albeit temporary,
trust fund that Social Security was projected to accumulate.

Sacred Cow

Depending on your point of view, the Old-Age and Survivors
Insurance Trust Fund, out of which Social Security benefits are paid,
is either one of the most important commitments of the federal government or a kind of monstrous con game.

Politically speaking, the former view has won out: Social Security is as close to a sacred cow in American politics as you can find. The last serious attempt to reform Social Security financing—by allowing individuals to invest their payroll tax contributions privately—crashed and burned in 2004, despite President George W. Bush spending considerable political capital on the issue. The more typical pattern has been bipartisan cooperation to improve elements of the program or correct missteps: in 1972, President Richard Nixon increased benefit levels by 20 percent across the board, which by 1982 helped lead to the near-depletion of the Trust Fund. In that year, a bipartisan Congressional coalition made a series of technical fixes to stave off the Trust Fund's impending collapse. The Trust Fund is still afloat, at least for the time being.

In key moments, both political parties have been invested in protecting the Trust Fund, which accounts for one of the oddest elements of Social Security, which is that even in this age of hyper-polarization, it somehow exists free from partisan political jeopardy. While there are many people who are deeply concerned about the long-term financial sustainability of Social Security, the most likely result is that this dynamic will continue, at least for the foreseeable future. Some analysts argue that, with a few modest changes to benefit and revenue levels, the Trust Fund's life can be extended from twenty to seventy-five additional years.[14]

1939 was the pivotal year in which the principle of funding Social Security through a Trust Fund supported by payroll taxes instead of general government revenues was firmly established. This represents an epic victory for Witte and Altmeyer. Recall that the goal in creating the Trust Fund was to set up a rough equivalence between contributions made into Social Security and benefits received. This was because they wanted Social Security to be understood as the public equivalent of a private pension plan (something the recipient earned as opposed to being given), and because FDR wanted it to be self-financed in perpetuity.

The word "rough" does a lot of work here, because in reality there's no way to precisely link contributions made into the system to money being paid out. In fact, in the early years of Social Security, recipients got a great deal—maybe as much as $10 received for every $1 contributed, given that they didn't pay into the program for very long before they reached retirement age. For many decades, there were so many workers paying into the system relative to people receiving benefits that the size of the Trust Fund could balloon. A Trust Fund surplus was confusing because it represented something counterintuitive: not so much a sign of robust health as an imperfect accounting of future liabilities, or money eventually owed to future recipients.

There is another way that Social Security was fundamentally confusing (and little understood), particularly in the early days. For early retirees, the deal was good because they got so much more money out of the system than they put into it. But to say the deal was "good" was only relative to the small amounts of money they were able to contribute through payroll taxes, not necessarily what they needed in order to maintain a basic standard of living. As we've written above, benefits in the early years were relatively paltry and certainly much less than what the Townsend Plan promised.

As liberal economist Paul Samuelson wrote in a *Newsweek* op-ed in 1967, Social Security was the "greatest Ponzi Scheme ever invented," because as long as the economy was growing and there were more young workers than retirees, beneficiaries would continue to get a good deal. Not to be undone, conservative economist Milton Friedman called it the "biggest Ponzi Scheme on Earth" because when the Trust Fund has a surplus, it doesn't just sit in a drawer somewhere—it is invested in US Treasury bonds, which in his view fueled reckless deficit spending by the US government. To Friedman, the Trust Fund was dangerous because it was a liability masked as an asset.[15]

The Battle of 1939

From the perspective of Witte and Altmeyer in the late 1930s, the situation looked different. They were focused on establishing the principle of individually funded insurance against income loss in retirement. In fact, they basically sought to remove Social Security from the realm of politics itself. This was the strategic value of likening the program to a private pension—it becomes something each individual owns, not a government program. That's why today you can go to the Social Security Administration website, plug in your information, and see what kind of retirement benefit you have "earned" through your contributions into the system. While it's sold as a retirement planning tool, in reality it's a living legacy to the program's founders, who wanted to frame people's understanding of Social Security in a way that was helpful to their cause.

This kind of strategic genius makes victory seem inevitable. But the intense battle over the 1939 amendments to the Social Security Act shows that Witte and Altemeyer's triumph was far from guaranteed.

FDR had insisted on last-minute legislative changes that would make Social Security deficit-neutral for at least thirty years. The practical consequence was that the Trust Fund would eventually generate enormous surpluses down the road. The prospect of these surpluses became, paradoxically, a rallying point for opponents of a payroll tax–funded program from both the left and the right.

For Townsendites, surplus was an obvious sign that the benefits being paid were ridiculously low. They besieged congressional offices with letters and telegrams demanding immediate changes. Another group of left-wing government officials, influenced by the British economist John Maynard Keynes, looked at this large sum of potentially available money as a lost opportunity to stimulate the economy. They believed it could be put to immediate use in the form of benefits when the economy was doing poorly and could be pulled back (in the form of reduced benefits) when the economy was heating up. (This would effectively mean that Social Security beneficiaries would have no idea what kind of benefit level they would have in retirement, which is why Witte and Altmeyer were opposed to the idea.) The chairman of the Federal Reserve Board, Marriner Eccles, blamed Social Security for the recession of 1937–1938, because of the combination of payroll taxes and insufficient governmental and private spending. (By 1939, the Trust Fund had already accumulated $390 million before a single benefit was scheduled to be paid.)

Republican criticism of the Trust Fund was even more vehement. According to Republican Senator Arthur H. Vandenberg, the Trust Fund was "the most fantastic and the most indefensible objective imaginable. It is scarcely conceivable that rational men should propose such an unmanageable accumulation of funds in one place in a democracy."[16] Republicans like Vandenberg believed that giving government a big pot of extra money to play with would inevitably invite reckless behavior.

For Witte and Altmeyer, these critiques from across the ideological divide posed an existential threat to Social Security. In a June 1938 speech, Witte remarked that "strangely the Left and Right are making substantially the same arguments" and that "radicals of all stripes want the benefits increased." To Witte, the real danger was still Townsend, because "once the concept is abandoned that the old age insurance system must be self-supporting," the result would be adoption of a "financially and socially undesirable . . . modified Townsend Plan."[17]

Their worry about a "modified" Townsend Plan was not that benefits would be absurdly generous in the short term but that they would inevitably regress to a much lower level, closer to the meager poor relief that Social Security was designed to improve upon. This was essentially what some Republican critics of Social Security were after: once a payroll tax–funded scheme was replaced by general revenues, it would be easier to control.

In late 1937, the Senate Finance Committee organized an advisory council to resolve these policy disputes. Witte was appointed as a member, and the council was directed to work closely with the Social Security Board, headed by Altmeyer. Characteristically, Witte "strongly advised his fellow councilors not to pressure for changes until experience had clearly shown a need for them," writes his biographer, Theron F. Schlabach.[18]

Ultimately, the pressure to reduce the Trust Fund surplus was too great to resist. The council's main recommendations were to start benefits earlier (in 1940 instead of 1942) while delaying the planned staged increases in the payroll tax from 1940 to 1943. The latter was particularly painful for Witte and Altmeyer, who believed that the payroll tax was the cornerstone to the program. (Congress would ultimately delay planned increases in the payroll tax until 1950.)

Congress eventually accepted the council's main arguments. Critical to Witte and Altmeyer, however, they made no mention of changing the funding structure to use general government revenues. The idea of Social Security as the public equivalent of a private pension plan survived. Witte and Altemeyer had lost some skirmishes, but they had won the fight that they cared about the most.

In her classic book *Policymaking for Social Security*, Martha Derthick calls this the victory of the "hybrid" model. She writes that "the slow-starting nature of social insurance served the program executives' long-run interest in achieving welfare goals (and) it served the legislators' short-run interest in keeping individual tax rates low." According to Derthick, it set a pattern that has helped determine the trajectory of Social Security to this day:

> In coming together to nurture this hybrid, the program executives and the "program" legislators in the committees did not so much agree on a purpose as a symbol ("insurance") and a process of policy-making—an incremental process. They agreed on a program the essence of which was that it would grow gradually and could be enlarged frequently in small steps at their own discretion. Both costs and benefits would creep up on the public; as costs and benefits grew gradually, the public could adjust to them gradually, and policymakers could judge the public's response as they went along.[19]

Derthick adds that in choosing the hybrid model, policymakers showed a "notable reluctance to debate fundamental premises and purposes, as their critics wished them to do." The notion of turning Social Security into a more transparent program funded by general revenues would recur in the years ahead, only to be swatted away by program executives. Observing that over time the link between taxes paid and benefits received became more and more tenuous, Derthick wryly notes that "the less like insurance it became, the more its executive leaders insisted that that was what it was."[20]

A Universal Benefit

Just how effective is Social Security as a poverty-fighting tool? According to the Center on Budget and Policy Priorities, very effective. They estimate that Social Security is responsible for lifting somewhere between 10 and 15 million elderly Americans out of poverty.

Put another way, between three and four out of every ten Americans aged sixty-five or over would have incomes below the poverty line if Social Security benefits were to be withdrawn. Social Security is a critical source of financial support for many elderly Americans. For about half of seniors, Social Security provides about 50 percent of their income; for one in four seniors, it provides 90 percent.

Given the racial and gender wealth gaps, Social Security is particularly important for Black, Hispanic, and female retirees, who experience higher poverty rates. This is in part because Social Security benefits are modestly progressive: for low earners, benefits replace about half of earned income versus a replacement rate of about 25 percent for higher earners. (This is the hybrid model in action, as higher earners receive a higher dollar amount in benefits, but a smaller amount as a proportion of their income.)

Finally, in a sign of the ultimate triumph for Witte and Altmeyer, Social Security is universal: according to Social Security Administration estimates, 97 percent of individuals aged sixty to eighty-nine either currently receive Social Security benefits or will receive it.[21] The long and sometimes painful process of incrementally adding more and more workers to the rolls has paid off.

After the tentative establishment of Social Security in 1935, the survival of a critical constitutional challenge in 1937, and the reassertion of the basic principles of the program in 1939, the Social Security Amendments of 1950 accomplished its founders' final goal of displacing its twin, the Old Age Assistance program. After long deliberation, Congress passed a series of amendments that added 10 million people to the social insurance rolls, including the self-employed, household workers, and farm workers; increased benefits by 77 percent; allowed payroll tax rates paid by employers and employees to go up from 1 to 1.5 percent; and increased the maximum amount of earned income to which the tax applied from $3,000 to $3,600.[22]

The 1950 Social Security Amendments followed a previous political pattern in that it passed under a Democratic president and a Democratically controlled Congress. However, as Derthick details, after 1952, this pattern would change, as Congress enacted major increases in Social Security benefits seven times, including under two Republican presidents, Dwight Eisenhower and Richard Nixon.[23] All told, between 1935 and 1990, Social Security benefits were modified a total of ninety-two times.

Witte and Altmeyer have each been called the "father of Social Security." They both disliked this honorific. In 1955, two years after his retirement, Altmeyer said in a speech: "I have been called the 'father of social security,' but what really happened was that I was the man on whose doorstep Ed Witte left the bastard." Tellingly, that quotation, reviewed by Witte's biographer as part of the archival material Witte retained, was crossed out, which may mean he never actually delivered that part of the speech.

It Ain't Necessarily So

In June 2021, Northwestern professor Daniel Immerwahr published an essay in the *New York Times* entitled "The Strange, Sad Death of America's Political Imagination." The subject of the essay was Edward Bellamy, a nineteenth-century author who called for a "radically different future." In 1887, Bellamy published a popular novel entitled *Looking Backward, 2000–1887*, which featured a man who falls asleep in 1887 and wakes up in 2000 to find an austere capitalist landscape replaced with a generous welfare state that included "universal education, guaranteed incomes and supported retirement." *Looking Backward* was the third-ranked bestseller of its time, nosed out only by *Uncle Tom's Cabin* and *Ben-Hur*.[24]

Immerwahr approvingly notes that FDR was a fan of Bellamy's novel and even published a book on the eve of his first inauguration in 1933 entitled *Looking Forward*. "The New Deal," Immerwahr writes, "seemed straight out of Bellamy." He compares this dynamic unfavorably to contemporary politics: "On both the right and left, activists call for things that, just a few years ago, would have been unspeakable. Yet rather than inspire voters, our politicians mostly seem to deflect or fend them off, seeing them as perhaps a little too inspired."

Let's take a brief dive into the plot of *Looking Backward*. In the novel, a young aristocrat named Julian West falls asleep in 1887 and is awakened in the year 2000 to a world that has been transformed into a socialist utopia. The government controls the means of production (there is no private industry) and everyone retires at age forty-five with a full and equal share of the nation's wealth. A college education is also guaranteed for every citizen. Under socialism, there are no more civil legal matters, and crime is committed by a small number of genetic outliers who are medically treated. When West is returned to 1887, he is horrified by the conditions of the time and cast out by his family when he tries to convince them of its inequities. The book ends when he realizes, to his relief, that his return to the nineteenth century is only a bad dream.

To put it kindly, the novel is long on vision and short on tactics and strategy. How to get from Point A to Point B is the question that politicians like FDR and program executives like Witte and Altmeyer wrestled with. They saw their job as an exercise in managing and overcoming constraints. FDR himself put it best in a 1938 speech when he said that there are "no shortcuts to Utopia."

One can imagine Julian West reacting much like Francis Townsend to the long, gradual gestation of Social Security: with fury and frustration.

The story of Social Security's first fifteen years goes a long way toward dispelling the mythology of the New Deal. In *Policymaking for Social Security*, Derthick identifies several reasons for the success of Social Security. The first was that to a remarkable extent, the program was directed by a small and stable group of system insiders, people like Witte and Altmeyer, who stayed involved over a long time horizon and were adept at navigating interest groups, advisory councils, and members of Congress. According to Derthick, "Policymaking is a compound of exciting, innovative events, in which political actors mobilize and contest with one another, and not-so-exciting routines that are performed without widespread mobilization, intense conflict, or much awareness of what is going on except among the involved few." Witte and Altmeyer were embodiments of the "involved few" and were masters of the "not-so-exciting routines."[25]

This relationship between ambiguity and elite professional control is summed up by Derthick, who writes that "In all, this was a hard program to classify politically, and a very hard program to understand." This ambiguity helped protect the program by making it harder for outsiders to come up with convincing arguments to change how it operated, since its technical details were difficult to comprehend by anyone other than a "highly expert few."[26]

Derthick also saw the downside of this kind of elite control: her book was published in 1979 when the Social Security Trust Fund was running dry. If anything, her fear was that the system's architects were too good at minimizing the basic political trade-offs (either cutting benefits or raising taxes) that sustaining the system required.

However, on balance, the behind-the-scenes, technical leadership by the "expert few" seems to have worked in the case of Social Security, leading to the program's gradual expansion over the years to serve almost the entire population of American senior citizens. In this case, it was the conservatives who were right to be worried about the incremental approach, not the radicals who favored a more immediate increase in benefits. As Derthick argues, had the social insurance model been rejected in favor of a program funded by general revenues, it would likely have been larger in the short term but smaller in the long run.

Perhaps the most important contemporary lesson that Social Security offers is a variation of the classic George Gershwin song "It Ain't Necessarily So." Today, there is a certain kind of circular logic at the heart of arguments about the importance of "bold" solutions to intractable problems. The theory is that change can only occur if broad social movements are activated and that in order to do so, leaders need to articulate clear and compelling messages. That is the basic idea behind "Defund the Police," or "Cancel Student Loans," or even "Stop the Steal." They have the same intrinsic appeal as Edward Bellamy's novel or the Townsend Clubs, but like them, they run up against the same limits.

This is not to say that enduring policy change is always successfully carried out by elect groups of policymakers engaged in incrementalism. As we showed in Chapter 1, our starting expectation should be that policy change is hard—and lasting change even more so. The word "necessarily" in the Gershwin song is important to keep in mind. Often incremental strategies crash and burn. But more likely than not, if you are, like Julian West, looking for the kind of change that would be immediately obvious if you woke up after being asleep for 100 years, it is likely to be the result of incrementalism.

Heroic Incrementalists

The case of Social Security is far from unique. Indeed, big social programs typically have to navigate a long and vulnerable period of gestation. In Chapter 1, we provided the example of the 2016 Toxic Substances Act, an update to a forty-year old piece of legislation that had failed to live up to expectations. Obamacare is another recent example. That story is told by journalist Jonathan Cohn in his recent book *The Ten Year War: Obamacare and the Unfinished Crusade for Universal Coverage.*[27] Cohn notes that Obamacare, signed into law in 2010, has followed a somewhat similar trajectory to Social Security in its first decade: a narrow constitutional escape, political jeopardy at the hands of a Republican Party committed to its destruction, and changes, such as the abandonment of the individual mandate to purchase insurance or the compulsory requirement that states expand Medicaid, that ultimately have not crippled Obamacare despite fears that they would. (Think of this as similar to Witte and Altmeyer's frustration about the repeated delays in planned payroll tax increases, which they feared might doom Social Security.)

Their success establishing the principles of Social Security from 1935 to 1950 make Witte and Altmeyer heroic incrementalists. Their heroism is all the more clear given their ability to fend off the well-meaning and seductive, but ultimately flawed, dreams of Francis Townsend, which threatened to destroy a program that began modestly but would eventually transform the lives of millions of Americans.

Witte and Altmeyer are exemplars of the kind of heroic incrementalism that today's political reformers should seek to emulate. Today, 60,000 employees work for the Social Security Administration, many at the Altmeyer Building in Baltimore, Maryland. If you go to the museum on the main campus, you'll find Altmeyer's words displayed prominently. In a kind of gradualist credo that sums up his life's work, the words read: "Social Security will always be a goal, never a finished thing, because human aspirations are infinitely expandable . . . just as human nature is infinitely perfectible."[28]

Social Security is a case study of intentional incrementalism—Witte and Altmeyer and their allies deliberately chose incremental reform when a bolder option was available. But not every government reform has clever technocrats like Witte and Altmeyer pulling the strings from behind the scenes. Sometimes incrementalism emerges more or less accidentally.

5

How New York City
Reduced Crime and
Incarceration

Four decades is both a long time and no time at all.

From one vantage point, nothing much has changed in New York City since the early 1980s. It is still home to millions of people who go about the daily work of living at a dizzying pace. As anyone who has ever spent time in the city can attest, the everyday hustle of life in New York can be overwhelming. Nothing comes easy. If New York City were to have an unofficial motto, it might be this one from Toni Morrison: "Talk shit. Take none."

The daily frenzy of activity in New York City brings with it a certain amount of conflict and disorder. And so, on any given day, the city's justice system is tasked with processing hundreds of cases, from minor misbehavior to major misdeeds.

If a visitor from 1981 were to step into a New York City courthouse today, he would find it instantly recognizable. Indeed, a visitor from *1881* might feel immediately at home. Superficially, very little has changed over the generations—the judges, attorneys, and police officers wear much the same uniforms that they have always worn and play the same roles that they have always played.

These surface similarities hide some seismic changes below the surface. Over the past forty years in particular, New York City managed to accomplish something that very few thought possible: dramatically improving public safety while at the same time shrinking the use of incarceration.

The crime reduction story has come to be known by a simple shorthand: the New York miracle. Whole volumes (and entire careers) have been devoted to explaining how New York was transformed from a city that felt ungovernable, where high levels of crime and disorder were perceived as an immutable fact of life, into the safest big city in the United States.

Less celebrated has been the accompanying reduction in the local incarcerated population. The number of New Yorkers behind bars, either in jail on Rikers Island or in upstate prisons, has been shrinking steadily for years. The city's jail population peaked in the early 1990s with a daily headcount of more than 20,000 people. Today it is around 5,500.

The typical New Yorker may not even be aware that this two-faceted success story of reduced crime and reduced incarceration has happened, but the impacts have been felt in nearly every corner of the city. Tens of thousands of New Yorkers have been spared the pain of victimization—either by crime or by the horrors of time behind bars. The ripple effects have benefited countless families and communities, making the city a better place to live and work.

In this chapter, we tell the story of New York City's underappreciated success fighting both crime and incarceration, a success that was accomplished thanks to a series of gradual improvements, each of which was basically undetectable to the general public, but that added up to significant change over the past forty years. We will also explain how this progress has recently been disrupted by seismic shocks to the system, in the form of sweeping legislation, street protests following the death of George Floyd, and a significant increase in the murder rate.

Escape from New York

Released in 1981, the film *Escape from New York* won no Academy Awards. It never appears on the "best of" lists compiled by august publications like *Film Comment*. The film was a minor hit, but it didn't shatter any box office records.

Nonetheless, *Escape from New York* did make an important contribution, one that was justifiably recognized by *Time Out New York* when it labeled the film one of the top ten movies ever made about New York.[1] While it is a work of fiction, few historical documents offer a more vivid depiction of how New York City was perceived at the start of the 1980s.

Set in the not-too-distant future (of 1997!), *Escape from New York* takes place in Manhattan, which has been transformed into a maximum security prison to deal with a 400 percent (!) increase in crime. As we explore the island through the eyes of our protagonist, Snake Plissken, we see that architectural landmarks—the World Trade Center, the New York Public Library, and the Queensboro Bridge among others—have fallen into disrepair. No place is safe. The streets are literally controlled by criminals, who sometimes emerge from underground to attack their prey. Vincent Canby, writing in the *New York Times*, described the setting of *Escape from New York* this way: "There are no services, no government, no work. The place is a random trash heap. Life is a permanent scavenger hunt, a nonstop game of hide-and-seek—when you're 'it,' you're dead."[2]

Escape from New York was hardly alone in depicting a city out of control, teetering on the brink of utter chaos. *Taxi Driver*, *Death Wish*, *The Warriors*, *Fort Apache the Bronx* . . . New York seemed to inspire dark and dystopian fantasies by the bushel in those days.

All of these films reflected a grim reality: New York was struggling. This was the era of "The Bronx is burning!"—Howard Cosell's famous exclamation (which he never actually said) when apartment buildings in the South Bronx went up in flames near Yankee Stadium during a World Series game in 1977.[3] This was also the era of "Fear City"—a name bestowed on New York by a pamphlet distributed at local airports in 1975 that warned visitors not to go out on the streets after dark.

Novelist Kevin Baker, writing in *The Guardian* years later, offered his firsthand testimony about moving to New York in 1976:

> It's difficult to convey just how precarious, and paranoid, life in New York felt around that time. Signs everywhere warned you to mind your valuables, and to keep neck chains or other jewellery tucked away while on the subway. You became alert to where anyone else might be in relation to you, augmented by quick looks over your shoulder that came to seem entirely natural. . . . *Everyone* I knew had suffered the violation of a home break-in. Worst was the idea that anything could happen, anywhere, at anytime. . . . There was a pervasive sense that the social order was breaking down.[4]

"During this period, many observers seemed to give up on New York," wrote Samuel Ehrenhalt of the Bureau of Labor Statistics, "having decided that the only course for the future was to manage decline."[5]

Historians point the finger for New York's declining fortunes at a wide variety of culprits—poor mayoral leadership, federal disinvestment, economic recession, and overambitious progressive reforms, among other malign forces. No matter who was to blame, there was little doubt that public safety was a big part of what went wrong for New York in the 1970s. Crime, including violent crime, had been on the rise throughout the decade. Echoing Nathan Glazer's famous *cri de coeur*—"Is New York City Ungovernable?"—many residents came to believe that crime in New York was, like the weather, beyond the reach of human intervention.

The wheels of justice in New York City continued to turn throughout the 1970s, to little discernible effect. In *New York, New York, New York*, Thomas Dyja describes criminal justice in New York as a senseless exercise in systemic ineffectiveness:

When a squirrely, harassed White commuter named Bernie Goetz shot four teenagers menacing him on the #2 train in December 1984, he found himself a vigilante hero, his feeling that "New York is out to get me" heard by many as an expression of their growing sense of futility: an estimated 1.7 million felonies committed in 1983 resulted in 22,000 convictions, meaning you had a 3% chance of ever getting punished for committing a felony, and 2% chance of doing time. Yet even with that, the State's prisons were filling up.[6]

Goetz was celebrated by many local residents for taking matters into his own hands. Other New Yorkers showed how they felt by voting with their feet. By the end of the 1970s, "Escape from New York" could have served as the title for the New York City census report— New York had lost 800,000 residents over the course of ten years.[7]

The Tipping Point

New York City in the 1970s and 1980s was a city in the grip of a crime epidemic. The number of murders in New York City doubled between 1970 and 1990, the year it peaked with 2,245 homicides.

And then, miraculously, crime began to go down, year after year after year. By 2018, there were fewer than 300 murders in the city. "New York had become the safest big city in the country," wrote Malcolm Gladwell in his best-selling book *The Tipping Point*. "It seemed hard to remember precisely what it was that (Bernie) Goetz had once symbolized. It was simply inconceivable that someone could pull a gun on someone else on the subway and be called a hero for it."[8]

The tectonic plates had shifted somehow. Crime went down not just in New York, but in cities across the United States. Analysts have pointed to an array of factors that were potentially at work, including a robust economy, declining rates of crack cocaine consumption, and a gradual recovery from the dislocations and social unrest of the 1960s. Economist Steven Levitt famously argued that *Roe v. Wade* was responsible—thanks to the availability of safe abortions, the theory

went, there were simply fewer unwanted babies to grow up into violent men. *Mother Jones* proffered a more elemental explanation: that
reduced exposure to leaded gasoline was responsible for the dramatic
decreases in crime.[9] And psychologist Steven Pinker speculated that
the reductions were part of a centuries-long trend away from violence
and toward more civilized behavior.

While crime went down in lots of places, the reductions were particularly dramatic in New York. Criminologist Franklin Zimring,
who wrote a book entitled *The City That Became Safe*, described what
happened as a "Guinness Book of World Records Crime Drop":

> New York's crime decline over the period 1990–2009 is so dramatic we
> need a new way of keeping score. Instead of talking about homicides
> dropping by 82%, another measurement is to ask how much of New
> York's crime rate was *left* by 2009? New York in 2009 had a homicide
> rate that was 18% of what it was in 1990, a robbery rate that was 16%, a
> burglary rate that was 14%, and an auto theft rate of 7% of the 1990 rate.
> *A 93% decline.* And NYC has remained essentially the same city—the
> population didn't change a great deal. But crime changed more than
> any big city under circumstances of social continuity where statistics
> were reliable than had ever before been tracked.[10]

What can account for success on this scale? While it is tempting to
look for silver bullet answers and heroic political figures, the truth is
less dramatic: the reductions in crime were the product of dozens, if
not hundreds, of changes made by police, courts, civic groups, nonprofit organizations, and other key stakeholders in the years since the
release of *Escape from New York*. "In the end, no one policy or person
ended crime as it was known in New York," declared Dyja in his history of New York.[11]

The first pieces of the puzzle were put into place by Mayor David
Dinkins. While the tabloid press treated him with thinly veiled contempt ("Dave, Do Something!" blared one infamous *New York Post*
headline), Dinkins presided over significant policing reforms. His
"Safe Streets, Safe City" initiative added thousands of police officers
to the force. The New York Police Department (NYPD) embraced

community policing strategies in an effort to bolster public trust. And a civilian oversight board responsible for reviewing complaints of police abuse finally became a reality after years of advocacy by progressive activists.

While murders peaked during the start of Dinkins term in 1990, crime went down in each of the following years of his term in office. These reductions accelerated during Rudy Giuliani's mayoralty. Giuliani's first police commissioner, Bill Bratton, was an aggressive reformer who, with the help of key deputies like Jack Maple, put a number of important changes in place. The first was CompStat.

CompStat was a performance measurement system that used computerized data to keep track of crime trends in each of New York's seventy-seven police precincts. Precinct commanders were regularly called into the NYPD headquarters at 1 Police Plaza to account for the statistics in their precinct. "What CompStat brought was accountability," Bratton claims. "It was hated by managers and cops alike for the fact that they are being held accountable, when for 20 years prior they hadn't been."[12]

CompStat encouraged police to identify, and concentrate their efforts in, "hot spots" of criminal activity. In so doing, CompStat built on the insight that crime does not spread evenly throughout a city or a given neighborhood—instead, it clusters in places that present unique opportunities for would-be criminals.

Alongside CompStat, the NYPD embraced another innovation that would prove to be much more controversial in the long run: broken windows policing. The broken windows theory, as initially articulated in an influential article in *The Atlantic* by James Q. Wilson and George Kelling, was relatively simple. Building on urbanist Jane Jacobs, Wilson and Kelling speculated that visible signs of minor disorder (like broken windows in a building) sent a message to potential criminals that a community was not being looked after, that no one cared. If left unaddressed, they argued that these conditions would eventually foster an environment of lawlessness that would lead to more serious offending.

The message that the NYPD, and many other police departments, took away from broken windows was not subtle. The police decided to enforce a broad range of "quality-of-life" offenses that had largely been ignored in previous years—public urination, public drinking, minor drug possession, and the like. Bratton first tested the concept in the subways, where he cracked down on farebeating and aggressive panhandling. "For the cops it was a bonanza," Bratton writes. "Every arrest was like opening a box of Cracker Jack. What kind of toy am I going to get? Got a gun? Got a knife? Got a warrant? Do we have a murderer here? . . . After a while the bad guys wised up and began to leave their weapons home and pay their fares."[13] While there was some variation from year to year, misdemeanor arrests in New York City increased by a whopping 190 percent from 1980 to 2013.[14] (Since 2013, thanks in part to concerns about over-enforcement, misdemeanor arrests have declined by 52 percent.)[15]

When they were first introduced, CompStat and broken windows policing helped to remake the public image of the NYPD. The department, which for decades labored to combat pervasive corruption within its ranks, started to seem like a dynamic, forward-thinking, and effective crime-fighting organization. But, over time, critics would argue that these two overlapping innovations would begin to calcify and curdle. Internal whistleblowers claimed that the demand to curb minor misbehavior and take crime stats seriously begat quota systems and ever-increasing demands for arrests.

More insidious still, in later years the same underlying logic would lead the NYPD to dramatically increase its use of "stop-question-and-frisk," a practice that enabled officers to detain, question, and frisk individual New Yorkers if there was a reasonable suspicion that they had committed, or were about to commit, a crime. In 2011, over 685,000 stops were made in this manner, most of them involving Black and Hispanic young men. In 2013, a federal judge would rule that the NYPD had employed "stop-question-and-frisk" in an unconstitutional manner. The numbers have gone down dramatically since then—to fewer than 14,000 in 2019, according to the New York

Civil Liberties Union.[16] But enormous damage had been done in the process, not just to the individuals who were needlessly stopped but to the relationship between the police and particular Black communities in New York City. These seeds would yield bitter fruit in the years to come, as we will see shortly.

As New York City got safer, policing innovations got most of the credit on the editorial pages and at the cocktail parties, but there were other changes taking place on the ground in the neighborhoods where crime had run amok in the 1970s and 1980s.

As sociologist Patrick Sharkey details in *Uneasy Peace: The Great Crime Decline, the Renewal of City Life, and the Next War on Violence*, a host of new nonprofit organizations emerged during the 1990s focused on strengthening neighborhoods and combating violence. Business improvement districts—organizations funded through special taxes on local businesses—supported additional security and community clean-up efforts. Community groups organized National Night Out against Crime events and other projects designed to reclaim city streets from those who would engage in illegal behavior. Youth development organizations offered after-school programming for at-risk teens. The list goes on.

No maestro was orchestrating all of this activity. There was no mastermind behind a curtain pulling strings. Instead, it was more or less a happy accident, with dozens of agencies and thousands of individual actors heeding a similar call—to help New York get back on track—in their own unique ways. The groups were not unified or even coordinated, but they were pointed in the same general direction.

For Sharkey, the crucial fact was that "urban guardians" of all sorts had multiplied—not just cops, but social workers, community outreach workers, local business owners, and others. To use Jane Jacobs's language, there were more "eyes on the street" than before, reducing the opportunities for crime and disorder. By analyzing data on every nonprofit organization that formed in the country's largest cities from 1990 to 2012, Sharkey and his doctoral students concluded that,

> As the number of community nonprofits rises, every kind of violent
> crime falls. . . . In a given city with 100,000 people, we found that
> every new organization formed to confront violence and build stronger
> neighborhoods led to about a 1 percent drop in violent crime and
> murder . . . the explosion of community organizations that took place
> in the 1990s likely played a substantial role in explaining the decline in
> violence.[17]

It seems that a virtuous circle was at work in New York City: more
public guardians led to safer streets, which encouraged more people
to come out of their apartments, which reduced crime still further.
By the end of the 2010s, New York had been utterly transformed. The
city that once was an international symbol of urban decay and lawlessness was now an unprecedented tourist destination and a magnet
for business investment. Subway ridership boomed. And neighborhood life was altered for the better in each and every borough.

Small Sanities

But the dramatic crime decline is just half of the New York story.
Contra the "tough on crime" conventional wisdom of the era, New
York also managed to dramatically reduce the use of incarceration
over the decades. According to Vinny Schiraldi of the Justice Lab at
Columbia University, "New York enters the 20s as not only the least
incarcerated, but also the safest, large city in the United States, with
incarceration rates that are a fraction of comparable cities and approaching the rates of other western nations."[18]

This success too had many causes.

The first, and most obvious, was that as crime went down, the
need to incarcerate New Yorkers was reduced as well. From 1989 to
2017, felony arrests in New York City decreased by 46 percent. This
translated into fewer people being admitted to state prison. Between
1984 and 1991, the number of city residents sent to state prison had
steadily increased to over 20,000 admissions per year. Since then, the

trend has reversed. In 2017, only 6,500 city residents were sentenced to state prison.[19]

Meanwhile, in the courts, two important developments were taking place, one pretrial and one post-adjudication. The pretrial shift was almost entirely invisible even to many people within the justice system.

After someone is arrested, if prosecutors decide to prosecute the case, an arraignment takes place in front of a judge. In New York City, many minor cases are resolved at this initial hearing—prosecutors and defense attorneys negotiate a plea agreement that is then blessed by the judge. But serious cases are rarely disposed in this way. In the parlance of the legal system, these cases are "continued"—adjourned for a later date, where prosecutors will have to present evidence and defendants will have a chance to fight their case. This raises a fundamental question: what happens to the defendant while the case is pending?

This decision is in the hands of the judge presiding over the case. Her choices can be boiled down to two options: out or in? That is, she can set the defendant free, with a promise to return to court for his next scheduled appearance. Or she can set bail, requiring the defendant to pay a set fee in order to guarantee his release. While some defendants manage to scrape together the money to purchase their freedom, many do not. These people are held in jail, which in New York City typically means the notorious Rikers Island jail complex, until their next court appearance.

So the rate at which judges set bail is a crucial determinant of the jail population: the more people who receive bail, the more people who will be held on Rikers Island. According to the New York City Criminal Justice Agency, in 1987, about 56 percent of defendants were released on their own recognizance, with no bail set, while their cases worked their way through the system. By 2018, this rate had gone up 76 percent. More than three out of every four people were leaving court without having to go to jail.[20] No one directed judges to change their behavior—they are all independent actors who make their own decisions. But change they did, in significant numbers. And the jail population went down as a result.

The other big change within the courts was initiated by two reformist chief justices, Judith S. Kaye and Jonathan Lippman, who together presided over the New York State judiciary for the years 1993–2015. Both Kaye and Lippman were committed to the idea of "problem-solving justice." They used their authority to create dozens of specialized new courts in New York City, including drug courts that sought to improve outcomes for individuals struggling with addiction, mental health courts that worked with defendants with mental health issues, and community courts that addressed misdemeanor offending.

Each of these courts was unique, but they all shared a desire to reduce the use of incarceration after someone had been found responsible for a crime. Instead of incarceration, the judges in these courtrooms tried to employ alternatives like drug treatment, mental health counseling, and community service wherever possible. Since their introduction in the early 1990s, New York City's problem-solving courts have handled tens of thousands of cases, contributing to the reduction in jail and prison sentences. They were aided in this work by an array of nonprofit organizations dedicated to providing alternatives to incarceration to New Yorkers. The political branches also made a contribution, reforming the punitive Rockefeller drug laws in 2009 in an effort to eliminate mandatory minimum sentences for drug possession and divert more cases to treatment.

All of these changes added up to a sea change in the administration of justice in New York. The reach of the justice system into the daily lives of New Yorkers had shrunk dramatically. Tens of thousands of New Yorkers who would have been in jail or prison—or on probation or parole—were instead free to go about their lives. With fear levels and jail numbers both down, activists began a campaign to close the jails on Rikers Island. Mayor Bill de Blasio and the New York City Council signed on, endorsing a plan to replace the jail complex with smaller, more humane facilities in four of the five boroughs.

Writing in the *New Yorker*, Adam Gopnik summarized what had taken place:

> Epidemics seldom end with miracle cures. Most of the time in the history of medicine, the best way to end disease was to build a better sewer and get people to wash their hands. "Merely chipping away at the problem around the edges" is usually the very best thing to do with a problem; keep chipping away patiently and, eventually, you get to its heart. To read the literature on crime before it dropped is to see the same kind of dystopian despair we find in the new literature of punishment: we'd have to end poverty, or eradicate the ghettos, or declare war on the broken family, or the like, in order to end the crime wave. The truth is, a series of small actions and events ended up eliminating a problem that seemed to hang over everything. There was no miracle cure, just the intercession of a thousand smaller sanities. Ending sentencing for drug misdemeanors, decriminalizing marijuana, leaving judges free to use common sense (and, where possible, getting judges who are judges rather than politicians)—many small acts are possible that will help end the epidemic of imprisonment as they helped end the plague of crime.[21]

Shocks to the System

Given all of the above, you might think that we are living through a golden age of criminal justice in New York City, a time when local residents are benefiting from an unprecedented peace dividend and law enforcement officials are enjoying high rates of public approval for their success in reducing both crime and incarceration.

But that, of course, is not how New York City feels as we write this in 2022.

The last couple of years have been tumultuous ones for the New York City criminal justice system. It has endured several major shocks to the system. The first came in the form of legislative change.

In 2019, the New York State legislature passed sweeping bail reform legislation eliminating money bail for almost all nonviolent felony and misdemeanor cases. Bail was to be restricted almost exclusively to violent felonies and even in these cases, judges were supposed to take financial hardship into account. In lobbying for reform, activists had effectively made the case that the criminal justice system was penalizing defendants for being poor—destitute defendants were being jailed while those with money to pay bail were being released. Controversially, the new law did *not* allow judges to consider whether someone was a risk to public safety in making a decision about whether to set bail or not. (Almost every other state in the country permits judges to do so.)

The new law was intended to reduce the number of New Yorkers detained in jail—and it did just that. Four months after its enactment, New York City's jail population reached a modern low of 3,800 people.[22]

Bail reform was the product of a significant shift in New York State politics. After years of divided government, Democrats had taken control of the Assembly, Senate, and governor's office. The influence of Republicans and conservatives was dramatically diminished. The bail legislation was a visible symbol of this new reality. The deference that previous legislatures had shown to law enforcement was out the window. Many New York judges, prosecutors, and police officials would subsequently complain that they had not been adequately consulted in the run up to the new legislation. (Practitioner veto warning!)

Almost immediately after the new law was enacted, the politics of crime in New York began to shift. The news media focused on several high-profile offenses, including hate crimes, that had been committed by defendants who had been released instead of jailed while their cases were pending. The New York City police commissioner Dermot Shea wrote an op-ed in the *New York Times* that summarized the feelings of many law enforcement officials: "New York's New Bail Laws Harm Public Safety."

The legislature rushed to respond to the criticism, amending the law in 2020. Despite the appeals of law enforcement officials, they resisted calls to allow judges to consider dangerousness when making pretrial decisions. Instead, the amendments simply expanded the list of charges eligible for bail and pretrial detention. They also allowed judges to impose programming on defendants accused of domestic violence.

According to the Center for Court Innovation, the amendments did have an impact, increasing the pretrial jail population by an estimated 7–11 percent.[23] But something else was at work too. As 2020 wore on, judges were setting bail more often. Not just by a little, but by *a lot*. At the time of this writing, the city's jail population is roughly 5,500 people. According to Tamiko Amaker, chief administrative judge for the New York City criminal courts, judges began setting bail more often because there was a marked increase in violence on the streets: "They're seeing one murder after another, or seeing one shooting after another, coming into their courtrooms."[24]

As Amaker makes clear, shootings have increased significantly in New York City since the original bail reform legislation passed in 2019. This reality has sparked an angry debate, with the NYPD and other opponents of reform claiming that the increase is tied to bail reform and progressive activists claiming that there is no evidence to tie the two together. Regardless of how one assesses these competing claims, the unfolding saga of bail reform in New York makes clear that increased crime is a real threat to the progressive reform agenda.

When all was said and done, two major changes to New York's bail statutes had been made in less than a year. Other significant changes ensued, including a vast expansion of a supervised release program in New York City that sought to offer some basic monitoring to defendants in lieu of nothing at all. The challenges of implementation were, if not an afterthought, certainly not a high priority for legislators. Frontline justice system practitioners—the judges, attorney, clerks, and others who are responsible for actually administering the system—were not brought into the process in a systematic way, and there was little, if any, room to adapt to their concerns and misgivings. Perhaps it should come as no surprise that, as crime increased, many judges were using whatever discretion they retained under the new law to impose money bail where they could in an effort to potentially detain defendants charged with violent offenses.

Even as the justice system struggled to deal with the implications of bail reform, it was confronted with an even bigger crisis: a wave of massive protests in the wake of the killing of George Floyd by a police officer in Minneapolis. And all of this was taking place in the midst of a public health emergency, as the city grappled with the implications of the Covid pandemic.

Although Floyd's murder took place hundreds of miles away, it resonated with a long and painful history in New York City. Over the years, a lengthy list of Black and Hispanic New Yorkers had found themselves on the receiving end of brutal treatment by the police, with many losing their lives in the process. Eric Garner, Abner Louima, Sean Bell, Eleanor Bumpurs, Michael Stewart, Amadou Diallo, Kiko Garcia . . . these names (and more) are reminders of a painful truth: the justice system still has a long way to go before it can be said to live up to the fundamental principle of equality before the law. The negative impacts of the system are felt most acutely by Black New Yorkers, who are disproportionately represented among both defendants and victims. This has been going on for a long time. For many Black New Yorkers, the justice system is the tip of a long spear, enforcing an oppressive and unjust social order.

Already angry, the protesters who flooded the streets of New York in the spring and summer of 2020 were further enflamed by a number of well-publicized cases of police misconduct as they attempted to manage the crowds. New York's season of unrest also included significant destruction and looting, particularly in parts of Manhattan and the Bronx.

With tensions running high, many local activists called for "defunding the police." From the start, the precise meaning of this slogan was slippery. To some, it was a statement about the need for a shift in spending priorities, away from law enforcement and toward social services and anti-poverty programs. For others, the meaning was more literal: they wanted to get rid of the police altogether.

The slogan succeeded in further enflaming passions on all sides. As the weeks passed and the protests died down, there was no return to normalcy. Something seemed to have broken between the police and the community. Several prominent politicians called for investigations to determine whether the police were engaged, intentionally or not, in a "slowdown," refusing to proactively make arrests. There was some evidence to suggest that the community had also retreated, becoming reluctant to call the police or serve as witnesses. According to the *Wall Street Journal*, the clearance rate for serious crimes (the percentage of murders, rapes, robberies, assaults, burglaries, and thefts that are solved by the police) fell by 26 percent from 2019 to 2020.[25]

All the while, shootings continued to rise—police reported an increase of 166 percent from April 2020 to April 2021, for example.[26] Disorder had also returned to the subways and streets of Manhattan. With fewer tourists and office workers thanks to the pandemic, the presence of homeless, addicted, and mentally ill individuals became much more pronounced. Public urination, drug use, and aggressive panhandling were a daily fact of life for those who visited Midtown Manhattan.

All this provided a backdrop for the Democratic primary for mayor in June 2021. Since Democrats far outnumber Republicans, winning the Democratic primary is tantamount to victory in most New York City elections. The crowded field (there were more than a half dozen credible candidates) began with candidates talking primarily about Covid-19 and economic recovery. It soon became clear that the thoughts of the electorate were elsewhere. Polling by NY1 suggested that crime was the top priority of Democratic voters. Remarkably, after a year of intense focus on police brutality and racism, 72 percent of voters said that they wanted *more* police on the streets.[27]

The mayoral candidates who embraced the rhetoric of "defunding the police" were mostly punished at the polls. Instead, the winner was Eric Adams, who would go on to defeat Republican Curtis Sliwa

to become the 110th mayor of New York. Adams was a former policeman, albeit one with a long track record of combatting racism
within the ranks of the NYPD. The first plank in his public safety
platform was a straightforward rejection of the defund movement:
"If we are for SAFETY—we NEED the NYPD!" He would go on
to say:

> Our city faces an unprecedented crisis that threatens to undo the prog-
> ress we have made against crime. Gun arrests, shootings and hate crimes
> are up; people do not feel safe in their homes or on the street. As a po-
> lice officer who patrolled the streets in a bulletproof vest in the 1990s,
> I watched lawlessness spread through our city, infecting communities
> with the same terrible swiftness of COVID-19.

This was the kind of messaging that helped to distinguish Adams from
the rest of the field. Many voted for him precisely because they did
not want to return to the "bad old days" of the 1990s. Bill Bratton, the
police commissioner who back then had helped bring CompStat and
broken windows policing to New York, exulted at Adams's victory:
"The good news is that at least in New York, at the top of government, there will be some sanity return," he said.[28]

★ ★ ★

The story of crime and incarceration in New York City isn't over, of
course. There will no doubt be twists and turns in the months ahead.
It remains to be seen whether Adams will succeed in his twin goals
of getting crime under control and reforming the miniature city-
state that is the NYPD. But, for the purposes of this book, two things
are clear.

First, an awful lot can be accomplished through incrementalism.
Over the course of four decades, public safety in New York was dra-
matically improved thanks to a series of reforms implemented by
the police, the courts, nonprofit agencies, and community groups.
As George Kelling explained in an essay entitled "How New York
Became Safe: The Full Story": "Only when a wide range of agencies

and institutions began to work on restoring public order did real progress begin."[29] This was accidental incrementalism at work. On their own, no single agency or reform was decisive, but together they added up to something significant.

Starting in the early 1990s, year after year, the crime rate and the jail population went down. By the mid-2010s, the city was utterly transformed.

They don't make movies like *Escape from New York* or *The Warriors* anymore. These days, the paradigmatic New York movie (for better and for worse) is probably *Sex and the City* with all of its glitz and glamour.

But much more than New York's public image has been altered. It is difficult to overstate the ramifications of the kinds of reductions in both crime and incarceration that New York has experienced over the past generation. Fear of crime was a fog that hung over the city, affecting almost every decision, including where to live, whether to invest, and whom to talk to. Hundreds of thousands of New Yorkers have been spared the pain of victimization and the harms of incarceration, enabling them to pursue their educational goals, their careers, and their family lives without encumbrance. The trajectories of countless families and communities have been markedly improved. In an era when many people doubt whether it is possible to address social problems, this kind of success should be broadly celebrated.

But the other lesson that the recent history of New York offers is more sobering: the gains of incrementalism are fragile. The imperfect planning for bail reform demonstrated a lack of respect for practitioners on the ground. The utopian call to "defund the police" shifted energies away from concrete reforms that had a chance to be implemented in the here and now and toward an abstract, philosophical conversation that was unlikely to be resolved any time soon. And the marked increase in shootings undermined many New Yorkers' interest in any criminal justice reform at all.

Incremental change may be the best way to make progress, but progress is never inevitable. In many policy areas, a two-steps-forward/one-step-back dynamic seems to be at work. Immigration policy is one such area. Nonetheless, it is also an area where, underneath the headlines, incremental changes have made an enormous difference.

6

The Immigration System's Hidden Strengths

If you're looking for a thorny public policy issue that the United States is handling well at the moment, immigration is probably not at the top of your list.

Concerns about immigration are arguably responsible for the rise of Donald Trump, who distinguished himself in the 2016 primaries by making outlandish comments ("When Mexico sends its people, they're not sending their best") and even more outlandish promises about building an impenetrable wall that would be paid for by the Mexican government. In the end, very little of the wall was built and President Trump was only able to make minor and temporary changes to the legal immigration system.[1]

Things are hardly better for Joe Biden, who campaigned on the promise of a more compassionate approach to immigration but has been sorely tested by a refugee crisis at the border and his sudden withdrawal of troops from Afghanistan, which left hundreds of thousands of Afghani nationals affiliated with American operations at risk unless they can leave the country.[2]

The Biden administration was clearly unprepared for the sheer number of individuals from countries like Haiti and Guatemala who have arrived at the US border. As a candidate, Biden criticized the Trump administration for drastically lowering the annual

refugee cap to 15,000 individuals, but, as president, he initially resisted raising the cap before reversing himself under pressure from
advocates.[3]

The sense of crisis at the border has been fueled by powerful and
heartbreaking images such as a US Border patrol agent on horseback
in Del Rio, Texas, grabbing a shoeless Black man by his shirt to prevent him from reaching a refugee camp. This left Biden exposed to
harsh criticism from the left wing of his party, for whom the image
invoked troubling comparisons to slavery.

For the blogger Andrew Sullivan, writing in October 2021, the
refugee crisis was a sign that Biden is "losing control of events." Sullivan
warned that Biden's continued failure to gain control of the border
would lead to the re-election of Donald Trump in 2024.[4] Supporting
Sullivan's claim, Biden's public approval ratings dropped in September
2021 according to an ABC News/Ipsos poll. Worryingly for Biden,
only 33 percent of respondents expressed approval of his handling of
immigration and the border situation.[5]

Given the polarization of the electorate, such low approval ratings
are striking. The best explanation is that both the left and right view
immigration as a failure for different reasons. But is this grim assessment fair? Is it accurate?

Closer inspection shows that immigration policy in the United
States is not reducible to a simple narrative of failure. In fact, from a
global perspective, the opposite is true: the ability of the United States
to attract foreign talent is the envy of the world. Indeed, other countries are trying to copy us—albeit with mixed results.

At the same time, there are clearly problems with the immigration system. It has obvious flaws, including the burdens imposed on
more than 11 million undocumented individuals and the 1 million
"Dreamers"—the children of undocumented immigrants who are
living in a state of legal limbo. (President Obama granted Dreamers
limited protections through executive order, but they can be rescinded
without congressional action.)

Another challenge is managing the populist backlash against immigration, which is not unique to the United States but has helped to fuel strong partisan divisions in the country. This is a difficult problem to address. Anti-immigrant sentiment tends to be strongest in the areas with the fewest immigrants, which means that it is as much a symbolic and cultural problem as it is a practical one. As such, it is not easily resolved by public policy.

Possibly the greatest obstacle to lowering the temperature of the debate is the fiction that immigration levels would be controllable if only the right law enforcement strategy were to be implemented. In many respects, immigration is not an issue that lends itself to government solutions. As we will show, at various points, the United States has attempted comprehensive solutions to immigration issues. These efforts have rarely been successful. And even when they have achieved their intended goals, the results have often been shameful, such as the openly racist 1924 Immigration Act.

To the extent that our immigration system has been a success, it has benefited not so much from good design but from the remarkable power of selection. Government policymakers set broad rules, but tend to defer key decisions about who gets to come into the country (and who doesn't) to employers, university admissions officials, immigrant family members, and (unintentionally) to immigrants themselves. The net effect of decentralizing crucial decision-making to people closer to the ground is that the country ends up with people who are more motivated to be here than if they were selected through a top-down process. In this chapter, we'll provide some evidence of the positive consequences of this kind of bottom-up process, which is a hallmark of the incremental approach to reform. Given the checkered history of comprehensive immigration reform in this country, and the hyper-polarization around this issue, incrementalism offers the most workable approach going forward to an exceedingly complicated problem.

A World Leader

"If the U.S. immigration system has so many flaws, how is it that it is more successful than any other country in attracting and integrating foreign talent?," asked an exasperated Chinese delegate listening to a lecture on the flaws of America's approach to immigration.

This story, told by Columbia University economist Neeraj Kaushal, helps ground the debate about immigration reform in a much different perspective than the inflammatory way the issue is often depicted in the media.[6]

First, a brief primer. About 3 percent of the world's population lives in a country other than the country of their birth. Despite reductions in the cost of travel and improvements in communications technology that make it possible to stay in touch with people back home, that 3 percent figure is basically the same as it was in 1900, 1990, and 2015. So while money and information are zipping around the world at a click of a mouse, immigration levels have stayed roughly the same for more than a hundred years.

About 45 million foreign-born people live in the United States, according to the Pew Research Center. That's close to one-fifth of all global immigrants. It's a big number, especially when you consider that second place Germany has only about 12 million immigrants living there. Still, as a share of America's total population, it's a little less than the proportion of foreign-born people who lived in the country in 1890.[7]

Three-quarters of immigrants are in the United States legally, including roughly 45 percent who have subsequently become US citizens and 30 percent who are either legal permanent or temporary residents. The rest, over 11 million people in all, are undocumented.

The United States grants about 1 million green cards per year. Despite the disproportionate attention paid to the refugee crisis, a relatively small number of immigrants are admitted as refugees in a separate program. (The numbers have ranged from a low of 15,000 to about 90,000 annually; while President Biden increased the potential number to 125,000 in 2021, delays in processing refugee applications might bring that number down.)

If you zoom out to the global level, what stands out is that countries like Japan, China, and most of Western Europe are in desperate need of more working-age people to fuel their economies, but they lack the administrative apparatus or the political will to change course—at least for now. "Countries are lining up to replicate the U.S. model," Kaushal writes, which includes separate and relatively well-functioning tracks for highly skilled workers, college students, and lower-skilled workers to come to the United States.

In 2019, more than a million international students were enrolled in US universities, twice as many as the United Kingdom and China, which rank second and third.[8] A program meant to attract high-skilled workers ran out of its annual allotment of 65,000 slots within a week, while a similar program in Germany was left unfilled for years. After decades of tinkering, the United States has recently increased avenues for the legal entry of workers from Mexico, leading to a dramatic drop in the number of undocumented immigrants from the country. (The current crisis at the Mexican border is largely focused on people from other Latin American countries, like Guatemala, who have to go through Mexico to get to the United States.)

In a description that will sound familiar to readers of this book, Kaushal writes that

> Failure to enact a comprehensive immigration policy (since 1986) has fed the notion that the U.S. immigration system is dysfunctional. This is not a fair description. In reality, almost completely unnoticed by the press, several smaller changes within the existing channels of immigration and temporary migration have addressed some of the deeper problems of the county's immigration policy.[9]

All told, immigration policy in the United States is an example of hidden incrementalism. If you look beyond the political and culture war headlines, it is even possible to find things to feel good about.

Selection, Selection, Selection

"As I tell my students, immigration in the United States is all about selection, selection, selection," says Kaushal.[10]

The most remarkable feature of the US immigration system is the broad dispersion of responsibility for who gets selected to come into the country. College admissions officers are a good example. There is a well-established system by which individuals from foreign countries can come to an American university. They have to apply and be selected to attend. For universities, foreign-born students are attractive because they often pay full tuition and thus can help subsidize domestic admittees.

Another example are employers, who have an obvious incentive to sponsor individuals who will be a good fit for their companies. Recruiting highly skilled software engineers has been crucial to the success of Silicon Valley, for example. Foreign-born citizens who are legal residents of the United States also sponsor family members and support them when they arrive.

Perhaps equally important, many immigrants control their own destiny. This is particularly true for undocumented workers, who bear enormous expense and risk to come into the country. Individuals willing to make the arduous trip to the United States typically do so because they believe there's going to be a job when they get there; they want to work and can make much more money here than in their home country. There is a fundamental link between immigration and the health of the economy: immigration flows pick up when the economy is strong and decline when it is not.

In sum, the United States continuously attracts talented people legally from across the globe. This is supplemented by the technically-illegal-but-mostly-tolerated process of bringing lower-skilled workers into the country at times when they are most needed. This is a description of a system that would likely not please anyone in the abstract, but it does have some important practical benefits, including for immigrants themselves who are seeking a better life.

The refugee crisis at the border understandably captures the public's attention and likely defines the mental image that many people have of the typical immigrant. But this ignores the usual way in which foreign-born people come to this country. "The stereotype of the illiterate, poor and rural migrant reaching the borders of affluent countries has to be abandoned," writes Francesco Castelli, a professor at the University of Brescia in Italy. "The poorest people simply do not have the means to escape war and poverty and remain trapped in their country or in the neighboring one."[11]

Foreign-born individuals in the United States help fuel our economy. They also help keep the overall US life expectancy from plunging to the level of poorer and more troubled countries like Ecuador and Tunisia. That is the conclusion of a study published in September 2021 by lead author Arun Hendi, an assistant professor at the Princeton School of Public and International Affairs.[12] According to the study, the life expectancy of foreign-born people who live in the United States is 81.4 years for men and 85.7 years for women, which compares favorably to world leaders Switzerland for men and Japan for women.[13] Overall, despite being only about 15 percent of the population, immigrants add about 1.5 years to American life expectancy on average.

Much of the current immigration debate betrays the so-called engineering fallacy: the idea that the right policy can bring the "right" people into the country. But these kinds of policies can only be set according to observable characteristics, such as how many years of schooling people have or whether they are wealthy enough to guarantee that they can be self-supporting. It's much harder for a bureaucrat to set up a system to pick people who are entrepreneurial, hard-working, and who take care of themselves. But that's just what the American system appears to do, without a centralized decision maker having to take on this impossible task.

Compared to What?

We are not arguing that the US immigration system is as strong or as humane as it could be. It would be fairer to say that the US benefits from comparison to the even more misguided approaches taken in other countries.

Japan provides a good example of the immigration-related struggles other wealthy countries are going through. With its shrinking and aging population, Japan desperately needs to attract younger workers to fuel its economy, but it is hampered by xenophobia. Japan's population is currently dropping by about 400,000 a year, driven by a low fertility rate. It has a higher share of people over sixty-five than any other country in the world (28 percent).[14] And there are reported labor shortages in every part of the country.[15]

Conservative governments such as those led by former prime minister Shinzo Abe have been able to increase immigration levels in the country, not by making humanitarian arguments but by stressing raw economic benefits. As a result, immigration levels tripled between 1990 and 2019, from a meager total of 1 million (out of a country of 126 million) to 3 million.

Yet compared to the United States, Japan struggles to retain immigrants. For example, Japan manages to attract foreign students to its universities, but over 90 percent leave the country immediately after they graduate. Consider nursing: Japan needs more nurses to take care of an aging population, but only 5 percent of foreign students are able to pass a standardized test that is administered only in Japanese. By contrast, according to Kaushal, somewhere between half and two-thirds of foreign students are working in the United States ten years after graduation.

The UK has also struggled to admit the immigrants it needs. In September 2021, the UK faced a critical supply crisis: gas pumps were bone-dry across the country. Limits to the flow of workers from across the European Union as a result of Brexit had led to an estimated shortfall of 100,000 truck drivers. Low pay and long-neglected facilities made it impossible to attract a home-grown workforce. Despite this crisis situation, Prime Minister Boris Johnson could only eke out 5,000 temporary visas to get foreign-born individuals (who were happy to take the job) back on the road. Even this small concession to economic reality was described as a major departure from Brexit-era norms.[16]

Across Western Europe, countries that combine generous welfare systems and strong labor protections are stuck in an unforgiving bind: they offer substantial welfare benefits but make it very difficult for immigrants to find legal employment. Almost the reverse is true in the United States, which has greatly limited immigrants' ability to access federal welfare and health care benefits while making it less difficult to find a job.

Canada's immigration system is often cited as a global model because of its transparency and because its highly structured point system has been able to attract a higher proportion of immigrants with a college or a higher degree than in the United States. (In describing their system, the Canadian government boasts "Come to Canada—The Right Way.")[17]

However, as Kaushal points out, upon arrival, immigrants who come to Canada end up earning less than purportedly less skilled immigrants in the United States. At the same time, the wage gap between foreign and domestic workers in Canada has grown—exactly the opposite of what happens in the United States. "Overall," Kaushal writes, "the Canadian point system gets more immigrants with observable skills like education but is less successful in admitting immigrants with skills that cannot be measured with common markers, such as motivation, creativity, imagination and enterprise."[18]

As the saying goes, imitation is the sincerest form of flattery. In 2015, Canada introduced the Express Entry program, which gives employers more authority to sponsor immigrants of their choosing. In 2020, they set aside about 90,000 slots for the Express Entry program, which is about as many as get into the United States through the H1B visa program, created by legislation in 1952. Express Entry is even marketed to individuals concerned about not getting into the US H1B visa program, a plausible strategy given how quickly the slots in the American program are exhausted.[19]

The Complicated Legacy of Comprehensive Solutions

As mentioned earlier, attempts to legislate solutions to perceived or real immigration problems have a spotty history in the United States.

A good example of this can be found in the three major pieces of twentieth-century immigration legislation, each of which is an example of a top-down attempt at comprehensive planning. Only one (the Immigration Act of 1924) achieved its original goal of dramatically reducing immigration levels into the country, but it did so shamefully: the legislation was unapologetically racist in its attempt to restrict immigration to a narrow band of Western European nations.

Two other important legislative acts, passed in 1965 and 1986, liberalized immigration but in ways completely contrary to their original intentions. The 1965 Immigration and Nationality Act was sold as an incremental measure but has completely changed the demographics of our country. By supercharging migration from areas of the world like Asia, the 1965 Act has made this country much more diverse. (It also made it much more difficult for people from Mexico to come to the country legally, up until relatively recently.)

The 1986 Immigration Control and Reform Act has also had a complicated legacy. While the act had the worthy impact of providing a path to legal residence for over 3 million undocumented immigrants, efforts to control entry into the United States have largely failed in the years since 1986. Moreover, the illusion that there is a law enforcement solution to movement across borders has helped set the stage for the current populist backlash about immigration.

The 1924 law, which greatly limited immigration into this country, has been treated very poorly by history. By imposing a country-by-country quota based on the number of foreign-born people in the United States in 1890, the law was unapologetically racist, with 98 percent of the quota spots held by countries in Western Europe. But it did work as intended: by 1965, the percentage of foreign-born residents in the United States had plummeted to just 5 percent from a high of 15 percent in 1890.

Jia Lynn Yang tells the story of the 1965 Immigration and Nationality Act in her book *One Mighty and Irresistible Tide.* As she writes, the law was the "culmination of a distinct, decades-long struggle" by activists and legislators like Emanuel Celler, who served as a member of the New York delegation to the US House of Representatives from 1923 to 1973. Their focus was on overturning country quotas, which during the height of the Cold War had become a millstone around the neck of the United States from a global public relations standpoint.

Advocates appeared to sincerely believe that abolishing the quotas would result in only modest change. In testimony leading up to passage of the bill, Attorney General Robert Kennedy testified that abolishing quotas in Asian countries would lead to about 5,000 immigrants coming to the United States in the first year, "after which immigration from that source would virtually disappear." This estimate was based on the backlog of Asian immigrants waiting for open slots, without taking into consideration that the preexisting quota levels were so low that few people had an incentive to get on the waiting list.[20]

In a good reminder of the danger of overconfidence in legislative intentions, an obscure conservative congressman from Ohio, Michael Feighan, secured a last-minute change that he mistakenly thought would largely preserve the mix of immigrants in the United States without the need for explicit quotas. His idea was to make the immigration system's top priority "reuniting families of United States citizens and permanent resident aliens."[21] The thinking was simple: because most foreign-born people in the United States in 1965 came from Western Europe, their friends and families would come from there as well. Feighan was so confident that the legislation exempted family members from the total number of people who would be allowed into the country in any given year.

For the bill's supporters, like Senator Edward Kennedy, this was an appealing formulation. Kennedy reassured the Senate that "our cities will not be flooded with a million immigrants annually.... Under our proposed bill, the present level of immigration remains substantially the same." As if concerned that the message was too subtle, he noted that "the ethnic mix of this country will not be upset" and the legislation "will not inundate America with immigrants from any one country or area, or the most overpopulated and economically deprived nations of Africa and Asia."[22]

As Yang writes, "the law's transformative impact would take years to reveal itself."[23] While initially the changes seemed modest, the ability of immigrants to invite extended family members over and above the overall cap led to dramatic changes over time. Yang cites a 1971 *Washington Post* article about a Greek immigrant who had already sponsored twenty-four family members. By that time, more Asians were entering the country than Europeans. All told, in 2019, over 700,000 people received lawful permanent residence (or green cards) through family sponsorship, a large share of the 1 million total green cards issued in that year.

According to a Pew Research report, without the 1965 change in immigration law, the United States would have been 75 percent White in 2015. Instead, that figure was 62 percent, with more than twice as many Hispanics (18 percent vs. 8 percent) and six times as many people from Asian countries (6 percent vs. 1 percent). In cities like New York and San Francisco, about one-third of local residents are foreign-born these days.

The initially slow-moving but profound impacts of the 1965 law continue to reverberate. The focus on family ties as a driver of immigration helps make the United States unique globally. Family members are responsible for two-thirds of all residency visas, more than any other country in the world. "In many ways the U.S. immigration system is a relic of the past," George Mason University professor Justin Gest told the *New York Times*. Gest, who studies comparative immigration policy, believes that the system "is far more generous than I think the spirit of the United States is today."[24]

Those opposed to family-based immigration have a negative term they use to describe this process: "chain migration." This is meant to call to mind an inexorable, uncontrollable process that threatens key American interests. But this critique ignores the value of making people already in the country responsible for helping new immigrants transition successfully. "There is a major undisputed advantage to family immigration," says Demetrios G. Papademetriou, cofounder of the Migration Policy Institute. "You have someone here who will show you the ropes, who will take you in (and) that can set up employment for you. When it comes to immigrant integration, family is very important."[25]

While the 1965 law ended up liberalizing immigration flow from Asian countries, it sharply curtailed opportunities for legal immigration from Mexico and other Western Hemisphere countries. Testifying to the complexity of the law's impact is Jane Hong, who wrote a *Los Angeles Times* op-ed arguing that the law "created illegal immigration."[26]

Prior to 1965, the "Bracero Program" (from the Spanish term for "manual laborer") allowed nearly 450,000 temporary entrants into the United States for seasonal farm work annually. In the early 1950s, even more people came into the country illegally in response to job demand. This led to a backlash. The dreadfully named "Operation Wetback" program established a militarized border in 1953. All of this was context for the 1965 law, which set the first-ever quotas on legal immigration from the Western Hemisphere. In 1976, entrants were capped at 20,000 per country, including Mexico, although family members of immigrants already in the country were exempt from that cap.

Depending on US labor needs, the number of immigrants who actually came into the country from Mexico could easily exceed this small legal allotment. As a result, according to Princeton sociologist Douglas Massey, "after 1965, undocumented migration was increasingly framed as a 'crisis' in the media and in public debates, portrayed either as a 'flood' or an 'invasion.'"[27] As with many aspects of the immigration debate, legislative choices have had unintended consequences and helped to dictate public perceptions.

The Fiction of Secure Borders

The Immigration Reform and Control Act of 1986 has had a similar history when you compare its impacts to what the bill's architects originally intended. The basic logic of the law was relatively straightforward: it provided a pathway for over 3 million undocumented workers to achieve legal status, while promising to control "illegal" immigration by punishing employers for knowingly hiring undocumented workers. As President Ronald Reagan said in a signing ceremony, the goal was to "humanely regain control of our borders."[28] Thirty-five years later, the consensus is that the 1986 law achieved its first goal (legalization of the undocumented) but miserably failed in its second (border control).

The law created a new requirement that employers verify employee citizenship documentation. Plagued by reports of fraud, an electronic employment verification system was introduced in 1996, which came to be known as "E-Verify." The E-Verify system is still largely voluntary, though rules vary from state to state and registration is required for all federal contractors and subcontractors.[29]

As Alex Nowrasteh explains in *Politico*, E-Verify is not much of an improvement on the previous version of the program for the simple reason that those in charge of administering it, including workers, companies, and politicians themselves, have rendered it "completely powerless." For one thing, the verification process is based on identification papers, which makes it easy to fool the system by submitting someone else's documents or fraudulent ones. Because it is still voluntary for many workers, employers can choose not to submit documentation or to look the other way when fake documents are submitted. For politicians, Nowrasteh argues, the E-Verify system offers an elegant solution: "Supporting it makes them look tough on illegal immigration while the fact that it's so easy to evade means their local businesses and economies are largely unaffected."[30]

This point was driven home in 2020, when the *New York Times* reported that the Trump organization was employing undocumented workers across its businesses, including individuals who "made Donald J. Trump's bed, cleaned his toilet and dusted his crystal golf trophies" at the Trump National Golf Club in Bedminster, New Jersey.[31]

The E-Verify system underscores the limits of law enforcement. To control immigration, policymakers had to rely on employers and immigrants to police themselves, but they didn't want to do it. Only something as drastic and draconian as the Immigration Act of 1924 has successfully limited immigration into the United States, but there's no chance that something that radical could (or should) be adopted today.

One response has been to increase the resources available to federal immigration enforcement agents. In 2003, the federal government consolidated immigration enforcement in a new agency, the Bureau of Immigration and Customs Enforcement (or ICE), within the newly formed Department of Homeland Security. Today, ICE has an annual budget of $8 billion and 20,000 law enforcement and support personnel.[32]

Even with these beefed-up resources, ICE has barely made a dent in the population of the undocumented: according to the Cato Institute, the Obama administration removed over 1.4 million people in the United States over an eight-year period. Those numbers earned Obama the derisive nickname "Deporter-in-Chief" from some immigration advocates, but year-to-year deportations declined from about 2 percent of the entire population of the undocumented in 2008 to six-tenths of 1 percent by 2016, when the Obama administration

changed the policy by focusing the attention of ICE on people arrested on serious offenses. Those percentages barely budged during
the Trump presidency, despite his bellicose rhetoric.[33]

The case for immigration law enforcement is ultimately more
political than practical. "There's still a lot of political support for enforcement," Kaushal says, "but not within the enforcement community itself," which is confused and demoralized about their ability to
meet their target goals.[34]

Even if the practical challenges of immigration enforcement could
be overcome, what would it cost to remove over 11 million undocumented workers from the country? Immigration hardliners should be
careful what they wish for. A 2015 study from the American Action
Forum estimates that it would require a new investment in ICE of
somewhere between $400 and $600 billion. The Forum also estimates
that this would have the broader economic impact of shrinking the
US economy by 6 percent, or $1.6 trillion, by the time the process
was complete.[35]

State and Local Solutions

Despite multiple efforts, no immigration legislation has passed in the
last thirty-five years that was as important as the acts introduced in
1924, 1965, and 1986. The most recent high-profile failed attempt was
by the so-called bipartisan Gang of Eight senators who succeeded in
passing a comprehensive bill through the Senate in 2013 by a 68–32
vote, only to have it stall in the House of Representatives.

This has not stopped legislative activity at the state level, however.

The National Conference of State Legislators has documented that
somewhere between 127 and 274 new state laws related to immigration passed every year between 2012 and 2020.[36] Tellingly, most of
those laws have sought to create a more immigrant-friendly environment within a given state. In fact, many such laws can be found
in states controlled by Republicans. An example is Michigan, where

Republican governor Rick Snyder successfully lobbied the federal government to provide 50,000 visas to highly skilled immigrants willing to commit to living and working in Michigan for five years. The law created a kind of ticket to legal residency in exchange for visa holders creating ten direct or indirect jobs in Michigan by making an investment in a new or existing company.[37]

Another example is Texas, which in 2001 became the first to offer reduced in-state college tuition to undocumented young people. Subsequent efforts to change the law have failed repeatedly, perhaps because of its economic benefits: the research and advocacy organization the New America Economy estimates that each new class of undocumented graduates (who have to have lived in Texas for three years and apply for legal status after graduation) provides $400 million in economic benefits to the state.[38]

This has led some observers to advocate for abandoning national solutions altogether and leaving it to motivated states and cities to compete for immigrant workers. In a 2015 *New York Times* op-ed entitled "Where to Go for Real Immigration Reform," University of Southern California professor Robert Suro argues that "a period of vigorous experimentation by state and local governments would be more productive than the polemics and stalemate that characterize the federal debate."[39] The basic idea is to take advantage of the American federalist system and let states and localities exercise their judgment about whether they want to welcome immigrants or not.

Since 1986, this kind of decentralized policymaking process has meant that immigration policy in the United States has taken on a decidedly incremental quality. The focus of the media is on polarizing national debates, but under the radar, hundreds of piecemeal solutions are being launched at the state and local level, including in some very unexpected places like Texas. In an ideal world, this process might help us to learn more about how to maximize the benefits of immigration for the economy, and for immigrants themselves, while minimizing opportunities for backlash and cultural disruption.

To be sure, there is a troubling trade-off here. Whatever their benefits, localized approaches don't offer a solution to national problems. But some advocates of liberalized immigration laws have shown that they are willing to make exactly this kind of a trade-off.

Take the issue of undocumented immigrants. There are more than three times as many people living in the country illegally than in 1986, when legislation created a path for legal status for over 3 million people. Creating a process whereby undocumented people could apply for legal residency would likely create not only a bureaucratic but a political nightmare. As Kaushal writes, "many immigration activists think that legalization would create more problems for the undocumented than they would solve."

Kaushal quotes a *New York Times* op-ed published by two economists, Jagdish Bhagwati and Francisco Rivera-Batiz, who argue that "if a comprehensive reform were passed, there is a serious danger that policy makers, operating on the flawed assumption that there should be no reason for illegal immigrants to exist, might enact harsher measures against them."[40]

The chances of seeing this dynamic play out in reality were reduced in September 2021 when the Senate parliamentarian ruled that attempts to legalize an estimated 8 million undocumented people would not be allowable under the "Build Back Better" reconciliation bill wending its way through Congress. For the moment, this effectively removed the controversial topic of mass legalization from the national agenda.[41]

Many immigration advocates were furious at the parliamentarian's decision (and at the Democrats for not seeking to override the decision). However, Kaushal argues that there might be a silver lining to this cloud, particularly for smaller pro-immigrant organizations who provide direct services to immigrants as opposed to larger national advocacy organizations. "They are interested in incrementalism," she says. "They don't want a huge thing that creates backlash."[42]

The Case for Immigration Incrementalism

Immigration provides an interesting case study because, as we have shown, the desire to move from one country to another is not easily controllable by government. There appears to be a relatively stable ceiling on the proportion of the world's population (about 3 percent) who are ready, willing, and able to take the momentous step of leaving home.

For all the vituperation of the current American immigration debate, the United States remains the top destination in the world for would-be immigrants. There are many reasons to be grateful for this. The economic benefits are clear: America needs immigrants to power its economy and make programs like Social Security (which depends on a favorable mix of working-aged to retired individuals) financially sustainable. According to the Bipartisan Policy Center, cutting legal immigration by 50 percent over ten years would result in a shortfall of $1.5 trillion in unfunded obligations by Social Security over seventy-five years.[43]

Welcoming immigrants into the country has led to a host of noneconomic benefits as well. Immigrants express high levels of pride in their American identity and in American institutions. As the freelance journalist Zaid Jilani (whose parents came to the United States from Pakistan) writes in *Persuasion*, "Immigrants are among America's hardest working and most patriotic people. They and their children are predisposed to love this country despite its flaws."[44]

As we saw in Chapter 1, the fact that Democrats and Republicans remain polarized about national solutions to immigration does not mean that nothing can happen. Beyond the headlines, there is a lot that all levels of government can do to improve immigration policy, provided that it starts with realistic expectations. Two goals would be to try to temper the populist backlash against immigration while looking for low-profile, technocratic adjustments to existing immigration rules.

The truth is that the US government has already shown that it can ameliorate problems at the border, however imperfectly. As mentioned above, the problem of "illegal" immigration from Mexico was in some sense artificially created by the decision to introduce entry quotas from the country in 1965. Between 2007 and 2016, however, the number of unauthorized people from Mexico in the United States declined by 1.5 million, the result of an increase in the number of visas issued and improvements in the Mexican economy, which kept more people at home.[45] That's one reason the more recent refugee crisis centers on people coming from other countries in the region like Guatemala and Venezuela.

Immigration offers us two important lessons. The first is that policies can create politics and not the other way around. For example, public perceptions about "illegal" immigration from Mexico have been largely shaped by discrete actions by US decision makers; when the United States lowered entry quotas below a realistic level, it helped to generate a sense of crisis at the border. Another example is the American commitment to a family-based system of immigrant entry, an artifact of what was essentially a legislative mistake, but which has led to the creation of a network of immigration advocacy organizations, often led by immigrants themselves, which are invested in protecting and extending the status quo.

As this chapter has repeatedly shown, the law of unintended consequences has been a regular feature of American immigration policy. Sometimes these unintended consequences have been positive, and sometimes negative. But little has gone exactly as planned—or forecast. Sometimes the best thing policymakers can do is to find ways to adjust to circumstances outside of their control. This provides a second important lesson, which is that policy debates should be more focused on addressing the complex legacies of past policies, particularly ameliorating harms, as opposed to imagining entirely new, idealized solutions.

There is still plenty left to do to ensure that we have a fair, humane, and effective approach to immigration in this country. An incremental approach to reform can help us take meaningful strides toward this goal.

Take the issue of unused green cards. This is the kind of low-profile, technocratic issue that is unlikely to become a flash point in the American culture wars. Every year, Congress allocates a certain number of green cards. Although there are always more applicants than there are green cards, sometimes the federal government does not issue every green card allocated for a given year, largely due to administrative errors. Congress has twice sought to reallocate these unused green cards, but it is estimated that at least 231,000 green cards remain unused. According to the Niskanen Center, relatively simple fixes by the executive branch and Congress could remedy this problem, enabling the government to meet the expectations of the original legislation.[46] This kind of fix might not answer the hot-button, abstract questions raised by immigration (What are our values as a nation? How should we prioritize among the various kinds of people seeing to immigrate to the United States—asylum seekers, skilled workers, family members, etc.?), but it would allow more people to legally obtain permanent residency, which would be a boon both to the individuals concerned and the US economy.

In sum, the history of American immigration policy suggests that incremental reforms (like figuring out how to use all of the available green cards that have already been authorized by Congress) can help us avoid contentious national debates and enhance America's ability to welcome immigrants to the country. It also offers plenty of examples of how centralized efforts at driving comprehensive change can backfire in unexpected ways. Those who want more evidence of the dangers of going too big, too fast should look no further than one of the most ambitious government undertakings in recent memory: the Great Society.

SECTION III

Stumbling toward Success

7

The Perils of Greatness

The assassination of President John F. Kennedy in November 1963 and the elevation of then-Vice President Lyndon Baines Johnson to the presidency created an unprecedented political opportunity. LBJ instinctively understood that he could advance an ambitious policy agenda by marketing his legislative package as a means of fulfilling Kennedy's unfinished legacy.

This rare window of opportunity opened even further after LBJ's landslide electoral victory over Republican Barry Goldwater in the presidential election of 1964, which also returned a two-to-one Democratic advantage in the Senate and increased an already substantial Democratic House majority by thirty-six seats. The so-called Fabulous 89th Congress would go down as "arguably the most productive in U.S. history," according to Karen Tumulty of the *Washington Post*, passing Medicare and Medicaid, the first federal investments in primary and secondary education, civil rights and anti-poverty efforts, as well as major immigration legislation (detailed in our previous chapter).[1]

Parts of LBJ's "Great Society" legislative program are justly celebrated. The Civil Rights Act of 1964 (which ended segregation in public places and banned discrimination in hiring decisions) and the Voting Rights Act of 1965 (which targeted racial discrimination in voting) addressed racist practices still in place almost a century after the end of the Civil War. These are two of the most important pieces of legislation ever to be passed by Congress. Medicare and Medicaid have also become permanent fixtures in American society, providing crucial access to health insurance to elderly, impoverished, and disabled Americans.

For ambitious people with ideas about remaking the world, LBJ's administration was an exciting place to work. Actually, feverish might be a better word for it. The gap between coming up with an idea and seeing it realized in practice was as small as it had ever been since the New Deal—and without a Great Depression–style economic crisis to limit horizons.

A central component of the LBJ legislative agenda was the "War on Poverty" that he declared in his 1964 State of the Union address. The speech led to the passage of the Economic Opportunity Act and the creation of Office of Economic Opportunity, headed up by Sargent Shriver (who was married to Eunice Kennedy Shriver, JFK's sister).

The Office of Economic Opportunity helped to launch and administer a range of anti-poverty programs, including Head Start, Job Corps, Volunteers in Service to America (VISTA), and the Community Action Program. This last program was to prove controversial. It was followed by another initiative, Model Cities, that attempted to improve on its predecessor. For different reasons, both programs would end up being largely perceived as failures.

Against the backdrop of more successful and enduring programs like Head Start, the rise and fall of Community Action and Model Cities is a cautionary tale. Tellingly, both were originally conceived in a potentially incremental fashion, as pilot programs, but in the cauldron of the War on Poverty, they were quickly supercharged beyond recognition.

Unlike the heroic incrementalists we profiled in Chapter 4, who were able to patiently build Social Security over multiple decades, the engineers of the War on Poverty sought to deliver immediate results in a complicated environment, in which overlapping government programs aimed at similar problems interacted in unpredictable ways. Their struggles should serve as a warning to anyone who wants to see government move quickly to achieve bold goals.

The Origins of the "Great Society"

LBJ is rightly remembered as a shrewd legislative tactician—the "Master of the Senate" in the words of biographer Robert Caro.[2] Yet perhaps what stands out most about his domestic legislative agenda was his self-confident belief that there was a government solution for every social problem.

LBJ's optimism was rooted in his personal biography. After graduating from college in 1928, he worked as a teacher in Cotulla, an impoverished South Texas community. His Mexican-American students were so poor that he would memorably recall "children going through a garbage pile, shaking the coffee grounds from the grapefruit rinds and sucking the rinds for the juice that was left."[3] (In 1965, when LBJ signed the Elementary and Secondary Education Bill into law, he did so in a signing ceremony alongside schoolchildren and their parents from Cotulla.)

LBJ's personal trajectory offers testimony to the power of national government action. After his teaching stint, he went to Washington, DC, to work as a congressional staffer. He soon became the Texas state director of the National Youth Administration, which provided employment to young people ages sixteen to twenty-five. He was elected to Congress in 1937 and immediately sought to emulate FDR by working to bring electricity to rural Texas.

LBJ was a man with a chip on his shoulder. He wanted to be taken seriously by the intellectuals and northern liberals who held enormous sway in Washington and the Democratic Party during the 1960s. He knew that they were suspicious of a southern Democrat from humble origins with a mixed record on civil rights and close connections to the Texas oil and gas industry.

LBJ decided to launch a charm offensive. He asked speechwriter Richard Goodwin, a former Kennedy aide who had clerked for Supreme Court Justice Felix Frankfurter, to come up with a "catchy phrase," like "the New Deal" or "the New Frontier," to help him advance his domestic agenda.

It was an awkward alliance. According to historian Randall Woods, Goodwin "would spend his nights ridiculing LBJ" on the cocktail party circuit and "his days working to shape the politics of the man who had usurped JFK." But it was Goodwin who seized on the expression "Great Society." He saw it as an overarching metaphor for LBJ's ambitious domestic plans. "My objective," Goodwin wrote in his memoirs, "was not to produce a catalogue of specific projects, but a concept, an assertion of purpose, a vision . . . that went beyond the liberal traditions of the New Deal."[4]

Many of LBJ's closest advisors were skeptical. They expressed deep concerns about Goodwin's draft of a major address that LBJ was to make at the University of Michigan in May 1964. They questioned how phrases like "individual dignity, identity, and fulfillment in a mass society" could be translated into a concrete legislative program: "It would be like legislating transcendentalism." In their view, LBJ was better off sticking to "bread and butter issues." They took a butcher knife to Goodwin's draft.

Goodwin fought back with the help of a young aide named Bill Moyers. Their winning argument, as Woods notes, was that the original version of the speech would help establish LBJ as a "man of ideas." As they declared in a jointly written memo to LBJ, it was "designed to make people like [James] Reston and [Walter] Lippmann [two prominent liberal editorialists] . . . sit up and say: 'This President is really thinking about the future problems of America.'"

LBJ delivered the Goodwin-Moyers version to near universal acclaim. It was interrupted twenty-nine times by applause. LBJ was deliriously happy with its reception.

According to historian Arthur Schlesinger Jr., Goodwin's visionary address represented a "clear victory of the liberal cause of American politics over the messianic conservative complex of the President's Texas mafia." In Schlesinger's terms, the "Texas mafia" saw the speech as a series of "dreamy vague proposals" that "would be interpreted as a hangover from the Soviet Union's series of unsuccessful five-year plans."[5]

Schlesinger was not far off in his assessment. LBJ's closest advisors didn't just dislike the speech, they disliked the very idea of presidential sloganeering. LBJ speechwriter and confidant Horace Busby tartly noted that JFK had achieved few of the legislative goals of the New Frontier and urged LBJ not to inflate expectations by giving his domestic ambitions a grand label. Busby and his allies "preferred to keep the administration's feet firmly on the ground," according to Joshua Zeitz, the author of *Building the Great Society*. They believed "the promise of good schools and access to medical care was lofty enough without faraway promises to fix humankind's broken spirit."[6]

The Professionalization of Reform

In the 1960s, intellectuals weren't just writing speeches. As author David Halberstam has argued, it was an era when "the best and the brightest" were exerting a powerful influence on public policy. "As never before, social scientists were actively engaged in the planning, and, later, in the evaluation of the programs of the Great Society," notes Brookings Institution scholar Henry J. Aaron in his book about the era, *Politics and the Professors*.[7]

Daniel Patrick Moynihan was one of many intellectuals who found themselves in Washington, DC, in those years. According to Moynihan, the United States was experiencing the "professionalization of reform." In his book about the War on Poverty, *Maximum Feasible Misunderstanding*, Moynihan includes social scientists, foundation executives, and a broad range of self-styled "experts" as being part of this emerging cadre of professional reformers. As he puts it, "the war on poverty was not declared at the behest of the poor: it was declared in their interest by persons confident of their own judgment in such matters."[8]

The LBJ administration was awash with presidential committees and blue-ribbon commissions. As Zeitz writes, "it was LBJ—not his predecessor—who fully leveraged the talents and imagination of the country's academics." At LBJ's urging, soon after the University of Michigan speech, Goodwin and Moyers went to Harvard and organized fourteen (!) different committees on a range of policy issues. Each committee was assigned a senior White House official as a liaison and "the output of their labors enjoyed wide circulation and consideration" within the Executive Branch. The product was a 1,400-page report for the president full of policy recommendations. And this was the abridged version.[9]

Moynihan had an ambivalent relationship to the professional reformers. A PhD in history, he was very much an intellectual (he would leave the Johnson administration to teach at Harvard and went on to serve many years as a US senator from New York). But Moynihan was also a skeptic of grand planning who had a deep appreciation for the working class. Raised by his mother in the Hell's Kitchen district of Manhattan, he admired the machine politicians of Tammany Hall because he believed they better represented the day-to-day needs and desires of their low-income constituents than more affluent liberal reformers.

Moynihan's concern was that intellectuals, while often "well intended," had "at most only a tentative grasp on a fantastically elusive reality." Their failing lay in not insisting "on the limits of their knowledge and methodology," particularly when they stepped out of their academic roles and into the realm of politics. Reflecting on his own status as a professional reformer, he wrote: "We constantly underestimate difficulties, overpromise results, and avoid any evidence of incompatibility and conflict, thus repeatedly creating the conditions of failure out of a desperate need for success."[10]

Moynihan would document this dynamic with the rapid rise of the Community Action Program.

The story of Community Action starts with a pilot project based in the Lower East Side of Manhattan in 1961 called "Mobilization for Youth." Funded by the Ford Foundation, the City of New York, and the federal government, Mobilization for Youth sought to ad-dress juvenile delinquency by expanding access to opportunity. The theory went something like this: young people in inner cities acted in antisocial ways because they lacked legitimate opportunities to fulfill their personal and professional goals. Summarizing the view of prom-inent academic sociologists of the time, Moynihan writes in *Maximum Feasible Misunderstanding* that the "delinquent is a normal youth with normal expectations that society does not permit him to achieve through normal channels." More concretely: "Lacking opportunity to earn money to buy clothes, he steals it."

For all of his paeans to moderation, Moynihan was no shrinking violet. He enjoyed the thrust and parry of intellectual debate and he had a way with words. His conclusion about the underlying ideas be-hind Mobilization for Youth was a typically colorful turn of phrase: "A half century of international sociology had produced a set of pro-positions not far from Father Flanagan's [the Catholic priest who was portrayed by Spencer Tracy in the 1938 film *Boys Town*] assertion that 'There is no such thing as a bad boy.'"

The launch of the Mobilization for Youth pilot was preceded by four and a half years of rigorous study and a 617-page document. "A plan," Moynihan writes, "devised by a group of middle-class intellec-tuals to bring about changes in the behavior of a group of lower-class youth who differed from them in ethnicity and religion, in social class and attitudes, in life systems, and above all, in life prospects."[11] The question Moynihan seemed to be asking—albeit with a mischievous glimmer in his eyes—was "what could possibly go wrong?"

What Went Wrong

When Sargent Shriver was tasked with formulating anti-poverty legislation in 1964, his immediate challenge was to resolve a dispute between two quarrelling internal factions, part of the task force of prominent academics and government officials organized by Goodwin and Moyers. One faction wanted LBJ to focus on a Works Progress Administration–style jobs program for young people. Another faction had something more ambitious in mind—giving poor people more control over anti-poverty programs.

LBJ gave Shriver six weeks to come up with a compromise, and Shriver came up with an emblematic Great Society–style solution: do both. With such a large legislative majority, there was greater emphasis on moving quickly than having a perfectly coherent plan. Before the end of 1964, the Economic Opportunity Act would devote $190 million annually to a youth job training program and $315 million to "community action" programs. Shriver was put in charge of the new agency that would oversee these new anti-poverty programs.

At least in theory, the Office of Economic Opportunity (or OEO) was dedicated to an ongoing process of trial, error, and discovery. "One of OEO's functions," writes Henry J. Aaron, "was to experiment with new programs, to run them long enough to determine their effectiveness, to terminate the failures and turn the successes over to regular federal endeavors, and then to move on to new endeavors." OEO recruited a number of bright economists and policy analysts "confident that analysis would confirm the value of at least a major portion of the new programs" while "jettisoning" the rest. This sounds a lot like how an incrementalist might approach the task of ending poverty.[12]

This did not prove to be in the case in practice, however. In the first year of the program's life, over 1,000 community action agencies received federal funding,[13] despite a recommendation by government officials that only ten demonstration areas receive initial awards.[14] The goal of patient, thoughtful experimentation had run up against the political imperative to get programs up and running as fast as possible so that they could have a positive impact in time for the 1966 mid-term elections. It was, after all, a lot of money; the $315 million devoted to community action programs was projected, by one estimate,

to create 125,000 jobs, which was higher than the number of ser-
vicemen in Vietnam at the time.[15]

From the start, OEO struggled to define the mission and scope of
the community action programs. In February 1965, the agency issued
a workbook for potential grant applicants that defined the goal as
"not merely improvement of the standard of living of the poor, but
a move into the mainstream of American life." How these agencies
should be governed was not exactly clear, but OEO wanted it to
involve nontraditional community groups and the poor themselves.
One example of an eligible program activity was "increased competence in protest activities"; OEO also encouraged local experimentation in "facilitating the opportunities for the poor to participate in
protest activities."[16]

With that much money to shovel out the door, there was a certain
slapdash quality to the program's early days. Charles Morris, whom
we met in Chapter 2, helped launch a community action program in
Trenton, New Jersey, as a young man in his twenties. Morris and a
small team were given two months to write grant applications to access a first round of funding. As he recalls, "All of us could write, and
we started grinding out program applications—everything we could
conceive of." They figured that at best they would succeed with one
or two applications. However, "in the space of about two weeks in
June, at first to our delight and then with something akin to horror,"
he wrote, "we received a string of telegrams informing us that essentially everything we'd asked for would be funded."[17]

Across the country, the combination of large sums of federal money
and the lack of clarity about how community action programs were
meant to interact with existing local government agencies produced
explosive effects. Mobilization for Youth would prove a harbinger of
what was to come. A few days before the passage of the Economic
Opportunity Act, the *New York Daily News* reported that nine members of the organization's staff had at one time been members of the
Communist Party. The article also suggested that a local activist, Jesse
Gray, had used office equipment to print up copies of a poster accusing

a White police officer of murder, a provocation which had allegedly played a role in sparking civil disturbances in Harlem. (Mobilization for Youth later confirmed that he had served as a "rent strike expert consultant.") Gray in turn accused New York City Council president Paul R. Screvane, the *Daily News*, and local landlords of attempting to discredit him.[18] Screvane later led an investigation into the agency's finances that resulted in the departure of the agency's executive director, as well as other reforms.[19]

A few months later, Chicago mayor Richard Daley exploded on a phone call with Bill Moyers, pointing out that government funding was going to a new community action program in Chicago, the Woodlawn Organization, that actively opposed the mayor's agenda. "Does the president know he's putting money in the hands of subversives?" Daley demanded to know.

In truth, community organizing was just one component of the community action programs. Many of these organizations provided a host of more traditional social services, like after-school tutoring, for local residents. But these kinds of activities did not generate nearly enough goodwill or attention to distract from the kinds of radical organizing that got community action programs in trouble.

The backlash to community action programs wasn't just a product of media sensationalism. Disgruntled local politicians had a point: the federal government was using taxpayer dollars in a way that posed a direct threat to them. As Connecticut senator Abraham Ribicoff pointed out, "setting up a new power base with the poor is absolute dynamite because it has led to anarchy."[20] To Ribicoff, the simple political reality was that to achieve his policy goals, LBJ needed the cooperation of the Democratic base, which included big-city mayors like Daley, labor unions, and other more established community groups.

The architects of the Community Action Program, and Congress itself, had a very different program in mind from the one that unfolded. (Remember Joseph Durlak's point from Chapter 2: "The program you think you are doing almost never turns out to be the program that actually occurs.") This was not particularly surprising, given that LBJ had given them only six weeks to come up with a plan and that, during its passage, Congress was consumed with other debates.

According to Moynihan, the ultimate fate of the Community Action Program was tied up in three words: "maximum feasible participation." The authorizing legislation called for the community action programs to provide for the maximum feasible participation of local residents. What did this mean? The UC Berkeley sociologist Lillian Rubin wrote that the congressional debates were "devoid of discussion about maximum feasible participation." A key Johnson administration official, Adam Yarmolinsky, would later say that his "conception of what it meant was that you involved poor people in the process, not put them in charge." LBJ seemed to have a similar notion, telling Mayor Daley, "Get your planning and development people busy right now to see what you can do for the crummiest place in town . . . we'll get our dough and then you'll have your plan and we'll move."[21]

But that's not how it played out. By the time hundreds of community action programs were rolled out across the country, it became clear that many of those charged with implementing the programs saw "maximum feasible participation" as a call to arms and a means of advancing a social revolution.

All of the ambiguities and tensions that would end up derailing the program were evident in the New York City pilot that started it all. Mobilization for Youth's budget for community organizing was fairly small, but, according to Moynihan, it "seems to have been the activity that most exhilarated the middle-class professionals" working there, with one official telling a reporter that "80 to 90 percent" of the agency's energies were spent "organizing the unaffiliated—the lower fifth of the economic ladder—who will overturn the status quo." City government was explicitly viewed as the enemy. "One dares to detect," Moynihan writes, "a measure of glee, almost, as the MFY theorists turned on City Hall, capitalism, racism, America itself."[22]

As in New York, so in the rest of the country. It didn't take long for local community action programs to spark political controversies in cities across the United States. As they did, political support for the program quickly shriveled. Community Action's budget was cut substantially in 1966. In the following year, Congress modified the original legislation to allow mayors and governors to assume control of local community action programs if they wanted to. Shriver would submit his resignation to LBJ in late 1967, after fighting multiple, bitter battles in cities across the country.[23]

By that time, LBJ and his advisors had moved on to a new solution to the problem of urban poverty: Model Cities.

From Community Action to Model Cities

Walter Reuther is one of the more interesting figures in the Great Society. Reuther was the head of the United Auto Workers at a time when unions were a particularly powerful political force in American life. He had a kind of Zelig-like quality. Over the years, he participated, in one way or another, in a wide variety of high-profile current events and policy debates. At one point he was dispatched by JFK to Cuba to negotiate a prisoner exchange with Fidel Castro. He played an instrumental role in creating the Peace Corps and in building support for the key pieces of the Great Society. He paid Martin Luther King Jr.'s bail when he was jailed in Birmingham, Alabama (where King wrote his famous "Letter from a Birmingham Jail"). He helped organize the 1963 March on Washington, speaking just before King's famous address.[24]

In late 1965, LBJ asked an aide to start working on a big new housing program, and the aide organized a task force (yet another!) composed of leading academics, business leaders, and public figures. Reuther was given a leading role. The initial mandate was to recommend new programs for LBJ's recently formed Department of Housing and Urban Development.

The task force's report focused on the shortcomings of prior federal government strategies—not just Community Action but the so-called slum clearance programs that were rapidly falling out of favor. Reuther believed that slum clearance took people out of their homes with the promise of better housing conditions but never delivered on the promise. He also thought federal programs were overly restrictive and gave local government too little flexibility. His strongest conviction, however, was that "federal aids were spread too thin to be effective," in the words of historians Bernard J. Frieden and Marshall Kaplan.[25]

The phrase the task force came up with was "Demonstration Cities" to denote the idea that investments should be made in only a handful of locations and that the normal rules for disbursing and spending government dollars should be suspended to allow for more flexibility and innovation.

In an unfortunate echo of the Community Action experience, the commitment to pilot testing and deliberate roll-out was quickly abandoned. In task force deliberations, Reuther advocated for a single demonstration: a rundown area of Detroit, where the UAW headquarters were located. An initial memorandum drafted by the task force suggested three sites. By the time there was a first draft of an official report, the proposal was for thirty-six sites, including six large, ten medium, and twenty smaller-sized cities. Task force member Senator Ribicoff urged that fifty additional small cities be added "so that members (of Congress) could feel that every single state might have at least one participating city." LBJ agreed, arguing that "to get demonstration cities through Congress, urban areas of all sizes and regions would have to be included."[26] By the time the final report was issued, the total number of participating cities was up to sixty-six.[27]

Total estimated costs for the Model Cities program was $2.3 billion over five years, of which the federal government would contribute $1.9 billion. As Frieden and Kaplan write, however, the task force gave "surprisingly little attention" to how Model City programs would interact with the existing federal grant programs in the cities that were chosen as demonstration sites, a critical issue that would grow in importance alongside the growth in the number of sites.

The basic idea behind the Model Cities program was to test whether a massive and coordinated infusion of federal aid in a concentrated area could reduce urban poverty. (Traces of this insight can be seen in more recent interventions like the Harlem Children's Zone, a much-heralded initiative that seeks to break the cycle of intergenerational poverty among local residents in Upper Manhattan.) The administrators of the Model Cities program would be working in cities that already had federal grants administered by numerous government agencies, which raised the obvious question of whether Model Cities would have control over how that money was spent. As with Community Action, the Model Cities task force did not articulate a clear vision about this crucial issue. The most generous interpretation of that silence is that they believed an infusion of new money would paper over the challenges of coordination: in addition to the $1.9 billion federal government commitment, budget officials calculated that a booming economy would free up an additional $4 billion in urban aid in forthcoming years. (Those same budget officials, however, did not take into account the growing cost of the war in Vietnam; the budgetary surplus would never actually appear.)

To the extent that they thought about these problems at all, task force members had what proved to be a misplaced confidence in LBJ's ability to resolve bureaucratic logjams. If LBJ could cajole Congress into passing major legislation, surely he could bend federal bureaucrats to his will, couldn't he? The history of Model Cities would ultimately suggest that "coordination" is not just an anodyne word—it is among the most persistent and thorny challenges for American government.

The Search for Superman

"Don't ever give such a stupid Goddamn name to a bill again," LBJ snapped at an aide in November 1966. LBJ was referring to the phrase

"Demonstration Cities." To LBJ, the word "demonstration" conjured up images of the kind of political radicalism that was undermining the Community Action Program. "Model Cities" was his chosen alternative.[28]

As he grew consumed by the Vietnam War, LBJ's naming intervention would prove to be the high point of his involvement in Model Cities. This was bad news for administration officials charged with rolling out Model Cities, because their ambitious goals would require some heavy political lifting.

As with Community Action, in its early days, Model Cities officials were overwhelmed by the process of soliciting and responding to grant applications from across the country. Even as the proposals were being drafted, little guidance was being offered about how to address fundamental challenges like how to define and enforce coordination across federal government agencies and what citizen participation could and should look like.

For many, a key component of Model Cities was its promise to restore power to local government agencies. A central criticism of the Community Action Program had been that it was unaccountable (and, indeed, actively hostile) to local elected officials. During the slum clearance era, many public housing and urban renewal programs had also been administered independently of duly elected mayors. One study in Oakland showed, for example, that only 12 percent of all federal money spent in the mid-1960s was under the control of local government.

Model Cities was meant to reallocate control over federal government spending to a single local government entity, but this turned out to be easier said than done. Early on, HUD (which administered Model Cities) made a play to take over control of the Community Action Program, which was housed within the Office of Economic Opportunity. This was rebuffed. HUD and OEO also spent time and energy trying to determine whether local mayors could effectively veto Community Action initiatives under the umbrella of Model

Cities. Perhaps predictably, the agencies issued contradictory (and self-interested) advisory opinions. This is not atypical—the quest for effective government coordination often runs aground over where the buck stops.

Urban renewal funding was another Model Cities target. This effort ran into similar problems. HUD tried to work with job training programs funded by the Department of Labor, but those programs had already agreed to be administered in cooperation with local community action programs in high poverty areas. Where there were disagreements, the Department of Labor regional administrator was supposed to have final say. Perhaps predictably, the Department of Labor was uninterested in surrendering this power to local government officials.

Citizen participation would prove to be another tricky issue.

While Model Cities sought to avoid the philosophy of maximum feasible participation that had caused Community Action such problems, citizen review was formally part of Model Cities application criteria. HUD's community participation expert, disappointed by the first round of Model Cities applications, began circulating notes to reviewers who shared a similar philosophy, noting that most applications did not include citizen groups in governance structures and urging that they be rejected unless this was corrected. As task force chairman Robert Wood said, "We let the genie of citizen participation out of the bottle with OEO programs, and now there was no way to put the cork back in."[29]

Eventually, HUD and OEO brokered a tortured arrangement whereby any disagreements on the direction of citizen action programming within a Model Cities jurisdiction would be referred to Washington for resolution. This prompted a heated attack from a national group of community action program directors, who called it a "document of capitulation" and threatened not to comply. (Practitioner veto alert!) As historians Bernard J. Frieden and Marshall Kaplan note in the *Politics of Neglect*, "Agreement had been reached in Washington, but it was a long way from taking effect in the cities."[30]

To resolve these difficult interagency questions, according to Frieden and Kaplan, HUD went into "Superman style," which they defined as making "comprehensive proposals that gave minimal attention to the conflicting interests behavior of other affected bureaus."[31] LBJ was their hoped-for Superman, but he had limited attention to bring to the challenges of implementation. "Members of the task force, in common with many of their contemporaries, had a naïve belief in the power of the President to reshape not only the federal government but the world outside Washington," Frieden and Kaplan write.[32]

By the end of LBJ's time in office, 150 model cities had been awarded funding. The program's core goals of concentrated funding and closer coordination were never achieved. Ironically, the congressional impulse to spread funding as far as possible helped keep the program going for years, including helping to defeat President Nixon's effort to zero out the Model Cities budget allocation within HUD entirely.

The ultimate judgment of historians about Model Cities would prove to be harsh. "Model cities was a noble dream," writes historian Randall Woods, but "there was no flood of new jobs, no new health and transportation infrastructures, few new housing projects and parks, little or no immediate relief. There was only the beginning of local political/administrative structures that would over the years hone their skills as grant writers and win support and trust from local residents and city halls alike."[33]

In their review of Model Cities, historians Frieden and Kaplan acknowledge that the goals of concentration and coordination were worthy ones. But they are clear-eyed about the ultimate lesson of Model Cities: "If the designers of future urban policies take away any single lesson from model cities," they write, "it should be to avoid grand schemes for massive, concerted federal action."[34]

The Loss of Innocence

It is important to place the failings of Community Action and Model Cities in context. Much was accomplished during the Great Society era. As Joshua Zeitz has written, "Few presidents have left in place so sweeping a list of positive domestic accomplishments. Fifty years after the fact, it is all but impossible to imagine the United States without Medicare, voting rights, integrated hotels and restaurants, federal aid to primary and secondary schools, or federally guaranteed college loans—all measures that continue to enjoy wide support."[35]

But there is also little doubt that LBJ's domestic program produced an enormous political backlash that would later contribute to the rise of Ronald Reagan. George Reedy, who served as Johnson's White House press secretary, came to believe that the sweeping promises associated with the Great Society "may have had a negative impact on the willingness of Americans to trust such efforts."[36] When the reality of programs like Community Action and Model Cities fell short of their own lofty rhetoric, many Americans came to embrace the argument, advanced by Reagan and others, that government itself was the problem.

Always attuned to elite intellectual opinion, LBJ would have been greatly perturbed by the common view that was articulated by Henry J. Aaron in *Politics and the Professors*: "Not only were the many programs of the Great Society oversold; they were under planned. . . . The result was a deluge of legislation . . . hastily enacted, and beyond the capacities of the federal or state government to administer."[37]

The perceived failures of the Great Society led to the disillusionment of a number of prominent liberal intellectuals, who ended up moving from the left to the right. "Neoconservative" thinkers like Irving Kristol, Nathan Glazer, and Daniel Patrick Moynihan (although he rejected the label) would spend years picking apart and condemning the more obvious contradictions and pretensions of the Great Society era.

Glazer's 1988 book *The Limits of Social Policy* represents an attempt to come to terms with the realization that professional reformers "seemed to be creating as many problems as we were solving."[38] Glazer came to the grim conclusion that much of what the government attempted not only failed, but was actually counterproductive.

Glazer's book is full of sobering observations about welfare reform (welfare rolls continued to swell despite attempts to provide income assistance to the poor), job training programs (which failed to make much of a dent in unemployment levels), and education (the persistence of substandard public schools, particularly in urban areas). Versions of these concerns continue to this day.

One of the paradoxical results of the "professionalization of reform" in the 1960s is that it led to a greater emphasis on policy evaluation and analysis, not all of which ended up being favorable to the aims of the Great Society. Perhaps the most prominent example is the Coleman Report, named for Johns Hopkins sociologist James Coleman.

The Coleman Report was issued by the Office of Economic Opportunity in 1966 in response to language in the Civil Rights Act of 1964 calling for a survey that would look at "the lack of availability or equal educational opportunities for individuals by reason of race, color, religion or national origin." Coleman and his team came to an unexpected conclusion: they found that the government spent an equal amount of money on public schooling regardless of race or the socioeconomic background of students. Coleman would argue that family background and motivation were the primary drivers of school performance, as opposed to teacher or school performance. It was family that mattered, not schools, according to Coleman.

The publication of the Coleman report was an "intellectual cause célèbre."[39] Given the findings—which directly contradicted the original purpose of the survey as defined by the Civil Rights Act of 1964— it's easy to see why the report caused such a stir.[40]

Henry J. Aaron was a critic of the Coleman Report and other similar research studies, which he disparaged for being methodologically flawed and (more fundamentally) "profoundly conservative" because large-scale impacts are unlikely to be found in research studies.[41] (For his part, Moynihan was prone to citing Peter Rossi's Iron Law of Evaluation that "the expected value for any measured effect of a social program is zero.")[42] Aaron ultimately came to reject the conventional thinking on both the left and the right: "neither the initial acceptance and enthusiasm for aggressive federal efforts to solve social problems nor the present rejection of and reticence about such undertakings are based on reliable information," he writes.

Aaron was writing in 1978. The optimism engendered at the start of the 1960s by President Kennedy ("One person can make a difference and everyone should try") had long since curdled. Successful moon shots had given way to urban unrest and unwinnable wars. The spirit of the 1970s was closer to Robert Martinson's grim conclusion about correctional programs: "nothing works." In the years since, we have come to a more nuanced place. We now know that some things work some of the time for some populations. (Of course, we aren't out of the woods yet—the replication crisis in social science has done a great deal to undermine confidence in research findings in recent years.)[43]

The Limits of Political Possibility

Community Action and Model Cities represented attempts to mold society to a preexisting vision—in the case of Community Action, a vision for how poor people could be more actively involved in decision-making processes, and in the case of Model Cities, a desire to reallocate power back to local government agencies which included folding disparate government activities under a single umbrella. Both programs failed to move the needle very much, despite huge government investment.

What can we learn from Community Action and Model Cities? One lesson is that existing power structures cannot be easily wished away. The backlash against community action programs by powerful local interests shouldn't have surprised reformers, but it seems to have done. "Just possibly," Moynihan writes acerbically, "the philanthropists and socially concerned intellectuals never took seriously their talk about the 'power structure.' Certainly, they seemed repeatedly to assume that those who had power would let it be taken away a lot easier than could possibly be the case if what was involved was *power*."[44] And as Moynihan notes, when the backlash did occur, the response by reformers was a kind of naïve shock: "One of the least attractive qualities of some of the early middle-class practitioners of conflict-oriented community action was the tendency to cry 'Foul' when the animal defended itself."[45]

Another lesson is to be mindful of the real-world challenges of coordination. Anyone who looks closely at American government will find overlapping jurisdictions and copious opportunities for conflicting mandates. Government entities have a tendency to engage in self-protection, protecting their turfs from those who would encroach, whether they are other government agencies or outside players like the community action programs. For this, and many other reasons, the search for greater coordination and collaboration often proves to be a false god.

A third lesson is that true incrementalism requires attention to political context. Community Action grew out of a single pilot, Mobilization for Youth, that was painstakingly constructed. The initial plan was to select ten replication sites. For their part, the advocates of Model Cities wanted to work out the kinks of a new approach to urban poverty in a handful of sites at most (or just one, in the case of Walter Reuther). However, the reality of congressional dynamics prioritized spreading programs over as large an area as possible to generate credit-taking opportunities for local representatives. The architects of both Community Action and Model Cities failed to see the potential dangers of moving too big, too fast. This may have been an understandable decision given the political dynamics of the moment, but both programs would end up paying a heavy price for abandoning incrementalism.

Community Action and Model Cities were in some ways different approaches to urban poverty. Community Action was intensely aspirational, the product of a unique moment of radical self-confidence within American government. Launched just a few years later, Model Cities represented a retrenchment of sorts. Recognizing the struggles of Community Action, it sought to respect and work within the confines of preexisting government agencies. Yet, as we have shown, Model Cities was in its own way equally unrealistic about the limits imposed by the local government context.

The common theme that unites both of these federal programs is that their adherents assumed that if something was politically possible, it was practically possible as well. JFK's assassination and LBJ's subsequent 1964 landslide election had removed the most significant political obstacles for Democratic reformers—the Republican opposition was small and in disarray. The economy was booming. The Democrats could justifiably claim a clear public mandate for change. And at the helm was the preeminent legislative politician of the day, the master tactician Lyndon Baines Johnson.

Despite all of these advantages, both Community Action and Model Cities would fall well short of their goals. The elimination of political constraints in Washington, DC, did not translate into success on the ground. This should provide a note of caution for those on both sides of the ideological divide who long for the removal of those constraints today.

8

The Four Core Values of Incrementalism

So far, we have tried to make the case that government should keep faith with gradualism as the best way to address social problems and combat injustice. We have explained the real-world obstacles that stand in the way of anyone attempting to achieve radical change in this country. We have documented some of the victories that incrementalists have managed to achieve over the years. And we have highlighted some of the risks that almost inevitably come along with attempting to go too big, too quickly.

In this chapter, we deal with a very real problem that stands in the way of widespread embrace of our argument: the fact that gradualism has become deeply unpopular among the chattering class in the United States.

In philanthropy, we are living through an era of "bold solutions" (e.g., the MacArthur Foundation's "Bold Solutions Network") and "big bets" (which *Forbes* described as "an-eight-figure-or-more attempt to create systemic social change.")[1] Our editorial pages, book reviews, and policy journals are also full of disrespect for incremental change:

The New Republic bemoans the "damp squib of incrementalism."[2]

In an essay entitled "Against Incrementalism," the *Boston Review* declares: "in a world recovering from a pandemic, facing a climate crisis, and beset by inequalities of race, gender, and class, small-bore solutions are a waste of time. Our only viable option is to have the courage to be ambitious."[3]

According to *The Guardian*, "This is no time for incrementalism. Only a radical program aimed at strengthening American democracy and preventing the return of rightwing minority rule in the future will rise to the moment."[4]

The Denver Post asserts: "Incrementalism has failed to protect Americans from the violence of racism."[5]

In November 2021, the *New York Times* devoted an entire special section of the paper to bemoaning "modest ambitions" in the United States. "It's time to dream big again," the paper of record announced, enumerating a series of "bold ideas" to "revitalize and renew" the country.

We could go on, but you get the picture.

Reading these, and other similar judgments, we come to an unavoidable conclusion: incrementalism is profoundly unsexy at the moment.

Peter H. Schuck, an emeritus professor at Yale Law School and the author of *Meditations of a Militant Moderate*, has devoted the bulk of his career to advancing a mode of thinking that he calls "fact-based, respectful of conflicting values, collaborative, solution-oriented." It would be difficult to find a more committed or articulate advocate of moderation and incrementalism. But even Schuck admits that his technocratic approach "is seldom exciting; it rarely makes the heart race or the spirit soar."[6]

The weight of conventional wisdom these days, at least among the cultural and educational elite, is decidedly in favor of radical change. (It is worth noting here that many ideas that are packaged as "radical change" are, upon closer inspection, actually incremental reforms.)

Incrementalism may represent a break from the fashionable rhetoric of the day, but we believe that, over the long haul, it is the best way to achieve significant change since it is more open to learning and adaptation and less likely to generate crippling backlash than initiatives that seek to accomplish "bold" change with a single fell swoop.

The incremental approach to change is rooted in the material world rather than in online echo chambers that privilege symbolism over substance. In finding a way forward, we believe it is essential to resist the lure of magical thinking that is disconnected from practical implementation. Incremental change offers a pragmatic path that can yield immediate dividends while beginning the difficult work of reunifying the country and restoring public trust in government.

In short, instead of bold schemes and utopian dreams, what is really needed at this moment of inflection in the United States is incrementalism. Our brand of incrementalism is rooted in four core values: honesty, humility, nuance, and respect.

Honesty

The United States is a remarkable country. Its scale, diversity, history of innovation, and founding commitment to liberal democracy all mark it as unique. As we have seen, it remains a magnet for immigrants from around the world.

Of course, the United States is also an imperfect nation, and has been from the start. It is a place where chattel slavery was sanctioned for generations. Where Black Americans have never truly received their due. Where extremes of wealth and poverty are not just tolerated but encouraged. As Kurt Andersen documented in *Fantasyland*, the United States is also a uniquely unhinged country, where violence, get-rich-quick schemes, and zealotry of various kinds have always flourished.

Any fair reading of American history and contemporary reality would catalog both the good and the bad—the founding genius, the tragic flaws, the historical echoes, and the halting progress we have made as a nation. But fair-minded, sober analysis is in short supply these days. Instead, many voices on both the left and the right have offered a distorted picture of reality in the United States.

The king of rhetorical bombast is, of course, Donald Trump. Examples abound: His claim that the media is the "enemy of the people," that American cities have been ravaged by "carnage," that the 2020 election was stolen, etc. etc. etc. Both as candidate and as president, Trump used his bully pulpit to exaggerate, lie, and vilify in a way that was unparalleled in recent American history.

Trump's escalation of political rhetoric was met with a very strong reaction on the left. According to Wesley Yang, author of *The Souls of Yellow Folk*:

> The Trump presidency radicalized America's governing and chattering classes. . . . The standards and practices that marked our professional classes as elites deserving of our trust in ordinary times (impartiality, procedural correctness) were no longer applicable. In a time of "literal white nationalists in the White House" putting "babies in cages," these protocols would in practice end up colluding with an existential danger. Departures from those practices become not just excusable but a moral imperative. Thus was undertaken a principled abandonment of scrupulousness in reporting, proportionality in judging, and the neutral application of rules once held to be constitutive of professional authority, all in favor of a politics of emergency. The new politics demanded loyalty and unanimity in an effort to defeat the usurper at any cost. The loss of proportionality in judging and scrupulousness in reporting created an echo chamber in which the bulk of the governing and chattering classes confirmed and exacerbated self-generated fantasies and fears of foreign subversion and fascists on the march.[7]

As Yang makes clear, we are living through an era of massive threat inflation. These days, it is not uncommon to see commentators compare overcrowded prisons to "modern-day slavery" or detention facilities at the border to "concentration camps" or abortion restrictions to *The Handmaid's Tale* or presidential elections to "Flight 93."

Robert Kagan's much-shared 2021 essay in the *Washington Post*, "Our Constitutional Crisis Is Already Here," is a classic of a genre that we call "the hysterical hypothetical." Kagan begins as he means to go on: "The United States is heading into its greatest political and constitutional crisis since the Civil War, with a reasonable chance over the next three to four years of incidents of mass violence, a breakdown of federal authority, and the division of the country into warring red and blue enclaves."

Once in the flow, Kagan's imagination really takes flight as he speculates on how a Trump campaign for president in 2024 might play out:

> The stage is thus being set for chaos. Imagine weeks of competing mass protests across multiple states as lawmakers from both parties claim victory and charge the other with unconstitutional efforts to take power. Partisans on both sides are likely to be better armed and more willing to inflict harm than they were in 2020. Would governors call out the National Guard? Would President Biden nationalize the Guard and place it under his control, invoke the Insurrection Act, and send troops into Pennsylvania or Texas or Wisconsin to quell violent protests? Deploying federal power in the states would be decried as tyranny. Biden would find himself where other presidents have been—where Andrew Jackson was during the nullification crisis, or where Abraham Lincoln was after the South seceded—navigating without rules or precedents, making his own judgments about what constitutional powers he does and doesn't have.[8]

Will Kagan's work of speculative fiction become a reality? We don't know. In fairness, it is not beyond the realm of possibility. Our point here is not to argue that Kagan is mistaken in his reading of the tea leaves, but rather to bemoan the impact that repeated exposure to the hysterical hypothetical has on our civic discourse. When every threat is presented as existential, when every opponent is a contemporary instantiation of Hitler, it becomes exceedingly difficult to perform the essential work of politics—establishing priorities, building consensus, and reaching compromise.

Not all of the blame for this rests on Trump's shoulders, of course. As we have described in Chapter 3, social media has played a particularly pernicious role, allowing partisans to separate themselves into tribal bubbles and rewarding outrageous content if it sparks engagement. In *Four Thousand Weeks: Time Management for Mortals*, writer Oliver Burkeman catalogs the effects of Twitter on his life: "It was impossible to drink from Twitter's fire hose of anger and suffering—of news and opinions selected for my perusal precisely because they weren't the norm, which was what made them especially compelling—without starting to approach the rest of life as if they *were* the norm, which meant being constantly braced for confrontation or disaster, or harboring a nebulous sense of foreboding."[9] Burkeman is describing the state of DEFCON 1 emergency that many of us seem to be living in these days.

Another force exacerbating the tendency toward permanent crisis is the professional incentives that dictate the behavior of many activists, politicians, and nonprofit leaders. We speak here from personal experience. In order to generate political momentum and raise money, whether from individuals, foundations, or government, it is often necessary to overstate the problems that you are trying to address. Between the two of us, we have played a part in writing hundreds of grant proposals and pitch letters over the years. They almost always begin with an attempt to frame the problem at hand in the most urgent terms possible. The result is a predilection for apocalyptic, end-of-days rhetoric that further erodes our collective sense of proportionality.

All of this adds up. Put simply, it is impossible to craft effective, responsive government interventions unless, as a collective, we can come to a clear understanding of the problems that we are trying to address. We need to be more disciplined in how we talk about our country's problems and take pains to guard against losing a sense of perspective.

But it is not just in defining problems where we need to be more honest. We also need to be more forthright about the solutions we are proposing. There are no silver bullets when it comes to addressing issues like economic inequality, ineffective education, and chronic homelessness. Indeed, as economist Thomas Sowell has argued, "There are no solutions. There are only trade-offs. And whatever you do to deal with one of man's flaws, it creates another problem. But you try to get the best trade-off you can get and that's all you can hope for."[10]

A less rancorous public square would acknowledge this wisdom. Almost any government intervention will also entail significant costs, both financial and otherwise. Values like quality and quantity, security and freedom, and privacy and transparency are typically in tension with each other—more of one will usually mean less of the other. Covid-19 has been a powerful case in point, as efforts to combat the virus through lockdowns and other measures brought with them real costs to our economy, social cohesion, and mental health. Getting the balance right is all but impossible if we refuse to acknowledge that there *are* trade-offs.

For all of these reasons, we would be wise to follow the advice that the civil rights activist and US congressman John Lewis once issued in an essay entitled "It's Time to Dial Down the Political Rhetoric." Lewis argued that "Toning down our rhetoric, respecting the dignity and worth even of our opposition . . . will demonstrate the spirit of the First Amendment and respect for the deepest meaning of the Constitution."[11] Channeling Lewis, we believe that honesty must be the foundation of incrementalism.

Humility

"We know what works to build safe and healthy communities."[12]

So declared the American Civil Liberties Union, arguing that policing should not be the primary response to criminal behavior. How many writers have uttered similar words over the years? Regardless of the topic, many opinion pieces can be boiled down to a simple argument: "we know what works and the only problem is that we lack the political will to implement these solutions."

If only it were that simple. The truth is closer to William Goldman's famous aphorism about life in Hollywood: nobody knows anything. The truth is that we do not know how to solve multifaceted, multicausal problems like poverty, oppression, and violence. Indeed, people of good faith have been debating how to solve these wicked problems for generations—and will likely continue to do so for generations to come.

It is estimated that over 100 billion people have lived on our planet. A great many of them have sought to eliminate human suffering. They did not succeed for a simple reason: the world does not easily conform to our dreams and desires, however noble they may be. Too many things get in the way, including bad luck and our own propensity for self-sabotage through error, avarice, and other means.

We have seen this dynamic firsthand in our work to reform the criminal justice system. More than a decade ago, when we were at the Center for Court Innovation, we worked on a project that sought to promote greater experimentation within the criminal justice system. As part of the project, we talked to dozens of leading criminal justice scholars and practitioners. One of our favorite conversations was with the late Joan Petersilia. The winner of the Stockholm Prize (the Nobel Prize for criminologists), Petersilia spent her career in academia but always sought to have an impact on public policy. At one point, she even embedded herself within state government in California in an effort to influence the state's prison reform efforts.

One reason we wanted to speak to Petersilia was that we had noticed that some criminal justice reform efforts that were launched with a lot of excitement seemed to peter out over time, leaving a sense of disillusionment in their wake. When we asked Petersilia about this, she said that there was "a long history of over-promising and under-delivering" within criminal justice. She went on to say:

> There's nothing in our history of over 100 years of reform that says that we know how to reduce recidivism by more than 15 or 20 percent. And to achieve those rather modest outcomes, you have to get everything right: the right staff, delivering the right program, at the right time in the offender's life, and in a supportive community environment. We just have to be more honest about that, and my sense is that we have not been publicly forthcoming because we've assumed that we would not win public support with modest results.[13]

As we argue elsewhere, we believe that modest improvements of the kind that Petersilia describes are not insignificant and that, over time, they can lead to major change. But it is also fair to say that many people are disappointed when they learn how difficult it is for government programs to move the needle.

This lesson was driven home quite forcefully some years ago when one of us (Greg) participated in a gathering that brought together all fifty state chief justices. At the conference, John Roman, a well-known researcher who was then at the Urban Institute, presented findings from a study that examined the impact of specialized drug courts that linked addicted defendants to drug treatment in lieu of prison.

The message that Roman intended to communicate was (mostly) positive: about half of the participants in drug courts successfully graduated and the programs had achieved statistically significant reductions in reoffending. In the world of criminal justice research, this amounted to a pretty remarkable achievement—very few programs are able to document *any* impact on the behavior of participants. Indeed, for many years the field labored under a cloud that "nothing works" to rehabilitate those who have committed criminal offenses.

If Roman intended to generate excitement among his audience, that's not what happened. A significant portion of the chief justices were dismayed to learn that only 50 percent of drug court participants successfully completed their treatment. Wasn't 50 percent a failing grade? These chief judges interpreted success as failure.

If some of our most highly educated professionals, operating at the very pinnacle of their chosen profession, are guilty of overinflated expectations, one shudders to imagine the disappointment of the typical voter when they think about government. According to Paul Gary Wyckoff, author of *Policy & Evidence in a Partisan Age*:

> Government policy is consistently oversold, to citizens, to politicians, and even to academics. It is oversold by both conservatives and liberals, in different but curiously similar ways. Over and over, we elect officials

in the naïve belief that they can pull some magic lever to fix our social and economic problems. When that doesn't work, we "throw the bums out" and elect someone to pull a different lever or to pull the same lever in a different direction.[14]

This is one reason why the calls for "bold change" these days are counterproductive. The language of "boldness," which implicitly frames policy disputes as contests between bravery and cowardice, runs the risk of continuing to foster disillusionment by inflating expectations beyond what government can reasonably deliver.

Make no mistake: we still need dreamers and visionaries and rabble-rousers who want to pursue moon-shot goals like curing cancer and ending hunger. But our default setting should be to admit the obvious: our problems are big and our brains are small. If we knew how to solve difficult social problems, we would have done it by now. A better civic discourse would acknowledge our limitations and commit to a process of learning by trial and error in an effort to build knowledge over time. That's why humility is central to our brand of incrementalism.

Nuance

As we documented in our chapter about immigration, in attempting to solve social problems, government must be mindful of the law of unintended consequences. One of the hallmarks of gradualism is an appreciation for the reality that any intervention that government makes is likely to create unanticipated effects. For example, Prohibition was a progressive reform that sought to reduce the manifold harms caused by alcohol abuse. But it ended up being repealed for multiple reasons, including the fact that it had the unintended effect of leading to a dramatic rise in organized crime.

The bottom line is that we should beware the lure of simplistic solutions. Our communities are complicated ecosystems that involve a multitude of moving parts. Reform efforts must be grounded in the complexity of human behavior and develop remedies that are as nuanced as the problems they seek to address.

But nuance is a difficult banner to march behind these days. Just ask Darren Walker.

Darren Walker is arguably the most influential philanthropist in the world. Named the president of the Ford Foundation in 2013, it did not take Walker long to make an impact at the august foundation, which has an endowment of $16 billion. Under Walker's leadership, Ford made an explicit commitment to advance social justice, even going so far as to rebrand their headquarters in Midtown Manhattan "the Ford Foundation Center for Social Justice."

In 2019, an issue of personal importance to Walker became front-page news in New York. A proposal to close the jail complex on Rikers Island and replace it with new, smaller, state-of-the-art jails located in four of the five boroughs was being debated in the New York City Council. Walker decided to use his bully pulpit to support the plan.

In an essay entitled "In defense of nuance," Walker decried extremism, which he labeled an "oppositional, nuance-averse posture" that "rewards ideological purity and public shame." About Rikers Island, Walker wrote:

> I am proud . . . to propose reasonable, workable solutions to shutter this warehouse of inhumanity and to end its long history of abuse and injustice. This was heavy lifting, full of competing interests and complexity—of nuance. Meanwhile, some advocates—including some community leaders who have moved the needle on criminal justice reform—oppose the construction of smaller, replacement jails, which will make the shuttering of Rikers feasible. . . . But we cannot let the perfect be the enemy of progress. If we skip steps, we risk creating a new kind of gap—a gap of missed opportunities and lost alliances.[15]

If Walker had hoped that his reasoned argument would spark thoughtful debate, he obviously hadn't fully absorbed the zeit-geist. Instead of introspection, Walker provoked rage among many of his readers. More than 300 academics (!), the bulk of them Ford

Foundation beneficiaries, demanded that Walker retract his statement and stop supporting the effort to build new jails in New York.
This was followed by a protest at his offices where dozens of activists
marched under the banner "Fuck your nuance."[16] When they arrived
at the foundation, participants chanted: "No more cages, no more jails,
Ford Foundation go to hell."

What was going on here? Why was a foundation that was dedicated
to advancing social justice and ending mass incarceration the subject
of such protest? The answers to these questions could be found in
the emergence of a new criminal justice reform coalition, No New
Jails NYC, that had staked out a position even further to the left than
Walker's.

While Walker's essay had acknowledged and celebrated the contribution that radical activists had made to the fight against over-
incarceration, No New Jails showed little patience for those who did
not explicitly endorse their abolitionist agenda, writing, "No New
Jails doesn't want anyone to be in jail. We are fighting for this outcome
over the course of many years, not capitulating to gradualist reforms
that abandon people to ruinous systems."[17] Many progressive New
Yorkers were inspired by this message, including Congresswoman
Alexandria Ocasio-Cortez, who provided the No New Jails coalition
with a high-profile endorsement.

The No New Jails protest at the Ford Foundation had no impact
on the ultimate outcome of the City Council vote (the plan to close
Rikers and build four new jails passed), but it was significant nonetheless. It signaled that the center of gravity in New York City politics
was moving quickly to the left. An idea that just two years before
had been seen as radical and impractical—closing Rikers Island—was
now viewed by many as not good enough.

More important, the "fuck your nuance" protest demonstrated how
difficult it is, even for someone with Walker's bona fides, to attempt to
promote nuance in our current media environment. Indeed, prominent intellectual voices explicitly argue *against* nuance these days. In
a 2018 *New York Times* opinion piece entitled "Does This Moment in

History Call for More 'Nuance,' or Less," writer John Herman argued that less was more: "This kind of subtlety is not of much use in politics, if we assume politics to be primarily about achieving power. A leader who recognizes nuance may be nice, but a nuanced campaigner is a bad campaigner; a nuanced speaker risks being misunderstood; nuanced proposals sound a lot like compromise."[18]

The Republican Party in recent years has been particularly averse to nuanced thinking. Their efforts at the state and local level to ban "critical race theory" and classroom instruction on sexual orientation and gender identity have been politically successful at some level. Certainly, they have put the Democrats on the defensive and generated a passionate response among the Republican faithful. But this political success comes at the expense of nuanced thinking and reasoned debate. How are we as a society to grapple with the complicated subject of how to educate young people about American history and identity if one our two major political parties effectively wants to stifle the debate by legislative fiat?

While activists on the right are the worst offenders, vociferous arguments against nuance have also come from those who see themselves as part of the resistance to the blunt politics of Trumpism. For example, in 2020, journalist Wesley Lowery famously tweeted: "American view-from-nowhere, 'objectivity'-obsessed, both-sides journalism is a failed experiment. We need to fundamentally reset the norms of our field. The old way must go. We need to rebuild our industry as one that operates from a place of moral clarity." While Lowery was offering a specific critique of journalism, this kind of thinking has also spread into academia, philanthropy, entertainment, and the nonprofit sector, among other professions.

The challenge, of course, is that on many, if not most, issues, it is not so easy to arrive at a place of "moral clarity." And even if "moral clarity" is somehow achieved, it is still possible for people of good faith to disagree about how this clarity should be translated into public policy. Even if we all somehow come to an agreement that we want to treat immigrants at our southern border humanely, the practical implications of this agreement are far from obvious. The devil is in the details.

Many (most?) of us long to be on "the right side of history." But this way of thinking suggests that there is a bright line between right and wrong. Things are rarely that simple. Ideas are not so easy to sort into clear categories marked "good" and "bad." Objectivity may be a platonic ideal that no human can ever achieve, but "moral clarity" is a false god that can easily lead to extremism and intolerance.

Rather than objectivity or "moral clarity," we should strive instead for nuance. For us, nuance means a commitment to moving beyond black and white, either/or thinking. It means acknowledging that social problems—whether it be homelessness or the opioid epidemic or the failure to provide high-quality public education for all school children—tend to have multiple causes and resist easy solutions. And it means making an effort to understand the real-world context in which problems occur and to learn from all of the relevant stake-holders, especially those with conflicting ideas. By embodying these tenets of nuance, incrementalism can help improve our public dis-course and give us a better chance of solving the problems that con-tinue to bedevil us.

Respect

While there is much about the future that we cannot predict, it is safe to assume that in our current political climate, almost every action that politicians on one side of the aisle take will generate a strong counterreaction from the other side. For those who participate in politics, policy debates are typically a zero-sum game: you win/I lose. Given this reality, any radical change is almost guaranteed to engender significant backlash.

In truth, partisanship has always been a feature of the American political system. There's nothing wrong with the clash of ideas—in fact, liberal democracy depends upon it. And, as many critics on the

left have pointed out, notions of "civility" have often been used co-
ercively, to silence marginalized groups and mute opinions that challenge the status quo.

Still, something feels different in our political discourse. The partisan attacks seem more intense. The epithets are more likely to be
ad hominem. And the identities of "Democrat" or "Republican" are
more fiercely held.

Partisans on both sides seem bent on demonizing their opponents. It feels unfair to Hillary Clinton to focus on a handful of
unscripted sentences that she uttered out of all the millions of
words that she spoke on the campaign trail in 2016, but her infamous comment—"You know, to just be grossly generalistic, you
could put half of Trump's supporters into what I call the basket of
deplorables"—struck such a deep chord because it reflected something very real: the contempt that many Democrats feel for Trump
supporters.[19]

This sense of disdain has only ratcheted up in the years since
Clinton spoke those fateful words. The Black Lives Matter protests,
the January 6 attack, the politics of mask-wearing . . . the Republican
response to all of these developments has understandably put leftists
on edge and, for many, confirmed their worst assumptions about their
political opponents.

On the right, the partisan animosity is, if anything, even more intense. The instinct to deride Democrats as "un-American" goes back
decades. Even before the social media era, right-wing voices on cable
television (Fox News) and talk radio (Rush Limbaugh) actively sought
to whip their followers into a frenzy. In recent years, Republicans have
often seemed more interested in "owning the libs" than advancing
substantive legislation. At the most extreme fringes, the right-wing
antipathy for the left is so fervent that it edges into some genuinely
scary places, including anti-Semitic conspiracy theories.

How do we get out of this box? How can we get to a place where
the political stakes are less dramatic, the fighting less personal, and the
discourse less toxic?

A good first step might be to eliminate partisan gerrymandering. In recent years, Republicans have engaged in particularly egregious redistricting in the states where they control the legislative process. While their efforts have been successful in the short term at tilting the political field in their direction, there have been significant long-term costs. Indeed, as conservative commentator George Will reports, many Republicans have become "scared of their own voters" and the ever-present threat of a primary challenge.[20] The creation of safe Democrat districts has similarly encouraged extremism on the left. An independent, nonpartisan redistricting process that creates genuinely competitive congressional districts could go a long way toward driving both parties back toward the middle (which also happens to be where most of the voters are, as we argue in Chapter 3).

Incrementalism has an important role to play in curbing over-the-top partisanship. Incrementalism suggests that any effort to advance change in the United States must communicate respect to ideological opponents—and work to incorporate their perspectives into the reform agenda. The concerns of 70 million Trump voters cannot just be waved away. (The same is true for Bernie Sanders supporters, of course.)

Unless our political parties are bent on the dissolution of the country, they cannot just force change down the throats of millions of Americans who object to, say, defunding the police or building an expensive wall along our southern border. That is a recipe for engendering backlash and further undermining our already badly frayed sense of national unity.

As we documented in Chapter 1 and Chapter 3, the country is less polarized than it sometimes appears. Congress does in fact pass bipartisan legislation on a fairly regular basis. And significant majorities of the public—Republicans, Democrats, and Independents alike—support a broad range of concrete reform ideas. We believe that our political parties should build on this foundation. Both Democrats and Republicans should take pains to craft agendas for incremental reform that reflect the interests of the majority of Americans rather than the most extreme voices at the fringes of each party.

Even if, as we showed in Chapter 1, extreme partisanship is more pronounced on Twitter and cable news than it is in real life, there is no doubt that, over time, polarization does have a negative cumulative effect, undermining a crucial democratic norm: respect for diverse viewpoints.

Both Republicans and Democrats acknowledge the importance of this value. According to a Pew Research Center study of political discourse in the United States, partisans on both sides of the aisle overwhelmingly say it is very important for elected officials in the opposing party to treat officials from their own party with respect. Republicans and Democrats alike both approve of compromise, at least in principle. That's good news. Less encouraging are Pew's findings that both Democrats and Republicans are much less demanding when it comes to members of their own party treating the other side with respect.[21]

Incrementalism rooted in respect for one's opponents is an approach that is available to anyone who is interested in speaking to the center of the American electorate. We hope that both Democrats and Republicans will heed this call because we believe that incremental change is the best way to help our country live up to its highest ideals—and to do so with the support of the bulk of the American public.

★ ★ ★

The four key values that we have articulated here—honesty, humility, nuance, and respect—are the values that have guided us as we have managed two criminal justice reform nonprofits, New York City's Criminal Justice Agency and the Center for Court Innovation.

We don't claim that these four values are some sort of magic formula. But over the years we have seen this approach win over skeptical criminal justice practitioners, bring together diverse audiences, and lead to concrete reforms that have improved the lives of thousands of people. This fuels our optimism that incrementalism can work.

In attempting to advance our own brand of incrementalism, we are inspired by the spirit of economist Albert O. Hirschman, one of the great advocates for improvisation and learning by doing.

Much of Hirschman's intellectual work was devoted to international development. He was alert to the dangers of preconceived notions and the seductions of planning led by experts from places like the World Bank. According to his biographer, Hirschman (echoing his brother-in-law, Italian socialist Eugenio Colorni) believed that "freedom from ideological constraints opened up political strategies, and accepting the limits of what one could know liberated agents from their dependence on the belief that one had to know everything before acting, that conviction was a precondition for action."[22]

For Hirschman, a reformist agenda, as opposed to a revolutionary approach, was the best way to grope toward progress given the inevitable limitations on our understanding of both the nature of the problems to be solved and the unpredictable consequences (both positive and negative) of change. He writes:

> While we are rather willing and even eager and relieved to agree with a historian's finding that we stumbled into the more shameful events of history, such as war, we are correspondingly unwilling to concede—in fact we find it intolerable to imagine—that our more lofty achievements, such as economic, social or political progress, could have come about by stumbling rather than through careful planning. . . . Language itself conspires toward this sort of asymmetry: we fall into error, but do not usually speak of falling into truth.[23]

What Hirschman is articulating in this passage is one of the reasons incremental reform has become unpopular: who wants to admit that we mostly stumble toward progress rather than boldly setting out to achieve it? But Hirschman is also underlining the promise and power of incremental change: we are in fact capable of making significant economic, social, and political progress—if we proceed incrementally.

Conclusion

The Endless Effort to Alleviate Injustices

The records suggest that Robert Moses and Jane Jacobs only encountered one another in person a single time (and then only at a public meeting), but they are forever linked in the history of New York City.

As immortalized in numerous books, films, and even an opera, Moses and Jacobs had conflicting visions for New York City. Moses was a master builder who, from the 1920s through the 1960s, was responsible for a series of massive public works projects that reshaped the landscape of New York, including bridges, parks, pools, playgrounds, and thousands of miles of highway. Jacobs thought more granularly. She championed what she called the "sidewalk ballet"—the intricate ecosystem that makes neighborhoods vibrant and livable.

They were, in many respects, perfect foils for one another: Moses was an Ivy League educated man and a doer—"Those who can, build. Those who can't, criticize," neatly summarized his worldview—who once held twelve different government offices simultaneously.[1] Jacobs, by contrast, was a woman, a critic, and a writer who never graduated from college and never held a position in government.

The paths of Moses and Jacobs converged in downtown Manhattan in the 1950s and 1960s. During those years, Moses sought to build an elevated highway in Soho and a road through Washington Square Park. Against the odds, Jacobs, a resident of nearby Greenwich Village, successfully marshaled a grassroots army to block Moses's plans.

The fight between Moses and Jacobs is typically depicted as a David vs. Goliath battle, with Jacobs cast in the role of the plucky underdog.

While Jacobs was hardly without influence or connections, Moses had access to the machinery of government in a way that Jacobs and her neighborhood allies did not. For this reason, Jacobs has traditionally been celebrated as an activist icon, fighting the powers that be on behalf of the voiceless.[2]

To us, Jacobs is something else: an incremental hero.

From our vantage point, the battle between Moses and Jacobs was a fight between comprehensive planning and incremental change. Moses, who began his professional life as a progressive reformer, was an advocate of "urban renewal." His ambitions for the city bordered on the utopian. He sought to change the physical landscape of New York City through large-scale initiatives and a top-down approach to planning. This involved a fair amount of destruction (aka "slum clearance") in order to make way for his vision of a rational, modern city.

Jacobs, on the other hand, had a more ground-level perspective. She was an advocate of mixed uses, short blocks, and the kind of density that facilitates safety by guaranteeing that there are always "eyes on the street." According to Jacobs, "There is no logic that can be superimposed on the city; people make it, and it is to them, not buildings, that we must fit our plans."[3] Building on this insight, she embraced spontaneity, complexity, and organic growth as opposed to master planning.

Jacobs is hardly the only incremental hero whose influence can be felt in these pages. In earlier chapters, we have highlighted the work of Charles Lindblom, Aaron Wildavsky, Daniel Patrick Moynihan, and Albert O. Hirschman. As we have admitted, we are neither philosophers nor historians, so we do not seek to offer a comprehensive intellectual history of incrementalism. Still, this book would be incomplete if we didn't shine a spotlight on three other key players who have played a particularly important role in advancing the idea of incremental change.

The first is Edmund Burke. Born in 1729 in Dublin, Burke served in Parliament for nearly three decades. In addition to being a statesman, he was a prolific writer and thinker, famous for his condemnation of the excesses of the French Revolution in *Reflections on the Revolution in France*.

Burke is sometimes dubbed "the first conservative" for his emphasis on tradition, his belief in the importance of property, and his advocacy of "little platoons"—family, church, community associations—that serve as a crucial buffer between the individual and the state.

But Burke's legacy has also been claimed by many liberals. According to Yuval Levin, "Burke's emphasis on gradualism . . . has appealed to some contemporary liberals eager to resist dramatic transformations of the welfare state. No less an icon of the American left than Barack Obama has reportedly described himself as a Burkean eager to avoid sudden change."[4] And political scientist Greg Weiner makes a powerful argument that we should consider Daniel Patrick Moynihan the "American Burke."

It is easy to imagine why Moynihan and Obama might be drawn to Burke, who was a cautious reformer, but a reformer nonetheless. At the heart of Burke's approach was an appreciation of complexity and a predisposition toward humility, pragmatism, and moderation. Crucially, Burke saw compromise as more than just a necessary evil: "All government, indeed every human benefit and enjoyment, every virtue, and every prudent act is founded on compromise and barter. We balance inconveniences; we give and take; we remit some rights, that we may enjoy others; and we choose rather to be happy citizens, than subtle disputants."[5]

Of course, Burke is not the only philosopher whose influence can be felt among those who embrace incrementalism. Another important guiding light is Karl Popper.

Popper, who lived for almost the entire twentieth century, was a fierce critic of totalitarianism, which he linked directly to utopianism. He recognized that human behavior was unpredictable and could only be molded so far by institutions, no matter how powerful. According to Popper, this "human factor" inevitably confounded the efforts of utopians, leading them, in the worst-case scenario, to attempt to alter human nature itself in their bid to transform society. "Freedom is more important than equality," he wrote, and "the attempt to realize equality endangers freedom."

Against utopianism, Popper sought to advance what he called "piecemeal social engineering." This approach emphasized attempting to solve social problems through small-scale reforms and a trial-and-error process that would lead to gradual improvement over time. According to Popper, the piecemeal method "permits repeated experiments and continuous readjustments." Humility was at the core of this approach: "the piecemeal engineer knows, like Socrates, how little he knows. He knows that we can learn only from our mistakes."[6]

Popper, who died in 1994, continues to be important to this day. His work has had a particular influence on George Soros, who labeled his philanthropy the Open Society Foundations after Popper's most enduring work, *The Open Society and Its Enemies*.

While Burke and Popper helped lay the intellectual groundwork for incrementalism, the Fabian Society has sought to translate incrementalism into pragmatic politics.

The Fabian Society claims to be Britain's oldest think tank—their motto, apparently presented unironically, is: "The future of the left since 1884."[7] The Fabian Society derives its name from the Roman general Quintus Fabius, who was known as "Fabius the Delayer" for his strategy of delaying attacks on the invading Carthaginians until precisely the right moment.

Originally formed by left-wing Victorians, the Fabian Society is devoted to advancing socialism and social justice through reformist strategies rather than through revolution. This approach is exemplified in the Society's original coat of arms, which featured a wolf in sheep's clothing. (We will not comment on the wisdom of branding yourself in a way that suggests that you are not to be trusted.)

Over the years, the Society has attempted to use the democratic process to move Britain gradually toward socialism. Along the way, Fabians helped give birth to the British Labour Party and advocated for important reforms like the establishment of the minimum wage and the creation of the National Health Service. Prominent Fabians include George Bernard Shaw, Michael Young, Clement Attlee, and Tony Blair.

The Fabian Society has had many critics over the years. Some have targeted specific failed ideas advanced by individual Fabians, like eugenics. More generally, the Fabians have been attacked on the right for their commitment to government intervention and on the left for not being radical enough. In *Whither England?*, Leon Trotsky dismissed Fabianism as "boring."[8]

Compared to What?

Incrementalism may indeed be boring when compared to more revolutionary approaches to change. But it does have the advantage of seeking to address three fundamental political problems: the world is complex, government decision makers are flawed, and, in a diverse democracy, there is rarely, if ever, widespread agreement about underlying principles or goals.

Recognizing these real-world obstacles, Charles Lindblom, the intellectual godfather of incrementalism, argued that if politics were a game of golf, the government should mainly use the putter, even for long distances. Lindblom also famously observed "a good policy is one that is agreed upon."[9]

Agreement, of course, is not so easy to come by in an environment defined by fierce partisanship, a multiplicity of special interests, and numerous decision points where different players can effectively veto new initiatives. Advocates of incrementalism suggest that, most of the time, the best way forward is to make piecemeal adjustments— and then to learn from experience before moving to make additional changes.

But if the status quo ante is fundamentally broken, this way of proceeding becomes less appealing. Over the years, the most enduring

criticism of incrementalism has been that it is a fundamentally conservative approach to change. According to this line of thinking, by
taking the existing status quo as a given, gradualism inherently limits the vision and ambition of government decision makers. Another
problem, from this perspective, is that gradual change will tend to
favor preexisting powerful interests that are well organized and know
how to manipulate the system.

Some critics have also faulted incrementalism's faith in the trial-
and-error process, pointing out that this kind of learning works best
when the benefits and costs of a given intervention are immediately
apparent. Unfortunately, sometimes the harms of a given approach are
only evident many years down the line. Climate change is the most
obvious example of this phenomenon.[10]

The battle between proponents of incremental reform and those
who favor more radical change is not a new one. As Thomas Sowell
explains in *A Conflict of Visions*, many contemporary political struggles
can be traced back to conflicting conceptions of the nature of humanity. According to Sowell, those who subscribe to the "constrained
vision" see humans as "tragically limited creatures whose selfish and
dangerous impulses can be contained only by social contrivances
which themselves produce unhappy side effects."[11] By contrast, supporters of the "unconstrained vision" believe that humanity is fundamentally good and that flawed institutions are to blame for problems
such as violence, inequality, and racism. (Jean-Jacques Rousseau is responsible for the most succinct expression of this idea: "Man is born
free but everywhere he is in chains.") Per Sowell:

> While believers in the unconstrained vision seek the special causes of
> war, poverty, and crime, believers in the constrained vision seek the
> special causes of peace, wealth, or a law-abiding society. In the un-
> constrained vision, there are no intractable reasons for social evils and
> therefore no reason why they cannot be solved, with sufficient moral
> commitment. But in the constrained vision, whatever artifices or strat-
> egies restrain or ameliorate inherent human evils will themselves have
> costs, some in the form of other social ills created by these civilizing
> institutions, so that all that is possible is a prudent trade-off.[12]

As Sowell suggests, incrementalism is a hard sell for those who espouse the unconstrained vision and believe that there is no reason why social evils cannot be solved. Similarly, if you think that the status quo in the United States is immoral and intolerable, you are probably not going to be convinced of the wisdom of incremental change.

Still, it is possible to offer a few responses to the criticisms that incrementalism is unambitious, slow, and a de facto endorsement of the status quo:

Incrementalism does not always mean small steps. An increment can be big or small. There is nothing inherent in the idea of gradual change that rules out large steps, so long as they are politically feasible.

Incrementalism is not necessarily slow. Indeed, because it seeks to lower the stakes, incrementalism encourages experimentation. Incremental reforms typically can be implemented much more quickly than comprehensive changes. Incremental experiments and iterative improvements can offer rapid responses to emerging social problems.

Incrementalism is not a defense of the status quo. To the contrary, incrementalism calls for ceaseless change. Critics of incremental change underestimate the power of the status quo and the influence of those who don't want any change at all. The American political system, which is characterized by checks and balances between branches of government and the diffusion of responsibility among local, state, and federal decision makers, creates multiple veto points where reform efforts can be stymied. Making anything happen is a challenge in this environment. And that's precisely what incrementalism does: it makes things happen.

But perhaps the most powerful rejoinder to criticisms of gradualism is simple: compared to what? There is an old saying, often attributed to Winston Churchill, that democracy is the worst form of government—except for all the others that have been tried. The same is true of incrementalism. The gradual approach has its flaws, but these flaws are minor compared to the flaws of doing nothing or the flaws of advancing transformative change in a single stroke over the objections of those who disagree.

Given the human suffering that continues to exist in the United States, doing nothing is untenable. The need for change should be obvious to anyone paying attention. In the face of injustice—of continuing poverty, discrimination, violence and more—inaction is a moral failure.

But, with rare exceptions, attempting to implement sweeping change is a recipe for disaster. The law of unintended consequences applies doubly to comprehensive reform: the larger the change, the larger the unexpected consequences. And genuine revolutions are generally to be avoided. In *You Say You Want a Revolution? Radical Idealism and Its Tragic Consequences*, Daniel Chirot argues that most modern revolutions have ended in bloodshed and failure. According to Chirot, "Once you unleash the forces of revolution, you make it possible for extremists of the right or left to take power, and their remedies most often turn into something worse than the original disease. That is not the case with gradual reform."[13]

Amara's Law

According to Michael T. Hayes, the author of *The Limits of Policy Change*, "The major drawback of policymaking in the United States is not that it is too incremental, but that it departs from incrementalism too often."[14] We agree. We also agree with Hayes that more work is needed to create the necessary preconditions that will lead to better incrementalism. In particular, we need to continue to try to level the playing field among various interest groups, so that the powerful do not drown out the weak.

But we see another looming threat to effective incrementalism: the danger of politicians whipping their constituents into a frenzy, demanding transformative change now. The siren call of the quick fix can be seductive indeed. The appeal of Donald Trump or, in a more minor key, proposals like Medicare for All or the Green New Deal or Abolish ICE, is that with one bold move, everything can change.

This brand of politics almost inevitably engenders disappointment and disillusionment. The big change almost never happens and even when it does, as in the case of Trump's election, the results are usually much less than supporters hoped for. Meanwhile, we spend less and less time thinking about the unglamorous, quotidian government decisions that actually affect our lives each and every day.

Given that we have written this book, at least in part, in an effort to push back against what we see as widespread catastrophizing in our public discourse, we do not want to over-egg the batter here. We recognize that politicians and pundits alike have been guilty of advancing big bang solutions and ignoring the nit and grit of everyday governing since the start of American democracy.

Still, there is something particularly undermining about this dynamic in the age of social media. Appearing on a panel to discuss "Moderation in an Era of Crisis and Extremism" in 2019, Elaine Kamarck of the Brookings Institution expanded on this theme:

> When politicians—year after year, election after election—promise the moon and deliver much less, it has a corrosive effect on democracy.... Social media has increased the attraction and the legitimacy of a set of ideas that, in fact, are simply not real. So to the extent that our political rhetoric diverges from the political possibilities, you really create an increasing distrust in the political class and a feeling that gives rise to forms of populism—a feeling that somehow the political class are corrupt, that there's something wrong with them. There's nothing wrong with them! I will tell you, having studied corruption around the world, that we have a marvelously uncorrupt governmental system. But in fact, the feeling of corruption is exacerbated when politicians go out there and say things that simply are not going to happen—and if they did happen, people would be up in arms.[15]

We believe that, in a world that is more complex than ever, incrementalism is more valuable than ever. Big change inevitably means big inconvenience. And big inconvenience means big backlash. Far from solving our problems, attempting to advance major change in a time of intense partisan conflict will only further threaten our already fragile sense of national unity.

Those who disagree with this assessment tend to argue that "We are not in an era of normal politics."[16] This argument is typically used to make the case that policy proposals that previously were dismissed as hopelessly utopian are now, in fact, politically feasible.

But, as we documented in Chapter 3, there is little, if any, evidence to suggest that the American public is interested in utopian visions. More than fifty years ago, social scientist Philip Converse famously argued in "The Nature of Belief Systems in Mass Publics" that, unlike elites, the vast majority of the American public has no clear ideology and little desire to develop one.[17] There is little evidence that the reality is any different today.

Ideological crusaders often fall into the trap of thinking that they are living in a revolutionary moment and that the standard political rulebook no longer applies. The Weather Underground in the 1960s and the Gingrich revolutionists in the 1990s both thought that they could dispense with politics as usual. They were both wrong. And they both did a lot of damage in the process.

Radical activists on both the right and the left are always looking for signs that they are witnessing a tectonic ideological shift in how the American public thinks about a given issue. More often, what is actually happening is a phenomenon known as "thermostatic public opinion." The public is simply reacting to the actions and rhetoric of whoever is in power and moving in the opposite direction. Under this theory, when government spending increases, the public reacts by demanding less. The reverse is true too: when government intervention decreases, the public demands more. The public is continually attempting to change the thermostat in an effort to get the temperature just right.

We are not arguing that incremental change is always and forever the best way of reforming government. There are moments of real crisis that demand more drastic change. But in an advanced democracy like the United States, these moments will be rare indeed. We do not believe we are living through such a moment. It is unlikely that the revolution is imminent.

That does not mean that change is not possible. Indeed, we believe that change is happening all around us. We have been fortunate to work in criminal justice reform in New York City since the 1990s. As we documented in Chapter 5, we have seen firsthand the impacts that incrementalism can have. Over the course of a generation, a series of incremental reforms led to historic reductions in crime and incarceration. New York City was transformed from an international symbol of lawlessness into the safest big city in the United States.

As we have seen throughout this book, seemingly small changes can yield large results over time. Social Security gestated slowly through a series of small steps over the course of fifteen years before becoming the largest federal program in the country. And a minor addition to immigration legislation in 1965 ended up changing the demographics of the United States, contrary to the expectations of the law's sponsors.

We often have a distorted mental image of government in the United States. Every day, local public servants are working hard, and in a collaborative fashion, to accomplish significant things. This news doesn't penetrate the consciousness of many Americans because there is simply too much competing for our attention. The dynamics of social media, which tend to favor posts that spark engagement (i.e., bad news), only makes this problem worse.

In our experience, the tectonic plates of government tend to move slowly, but they do move. Over time, seemingly modest changes add up. These improvements don't have to be sexy. It could be streamlining a bureaucratic process or fine-tuning the tax code or finding a little more money to support an effective community program. We believe that the little things matter.

When it comes to government reform, our North Star should be Amara's Law. This is an insight that is attributed to Roy Amara, a Stanford University computer scientist who for many years served as the head of the beguilingly named "Institute for the Future." Amara's Law argues that we tend to overestimate what can be accomplished in the short term and underestimate what can be done in the long term.

As Amara's Law suggests, it is easy to underestimate what we have accomplished in the United States. For all its flaws, our political system is a reasonably stable, functioning democracy that has managed to keep a diverse nation of 330 million people moving forward. Many Americans take for granted achievements, like the rule of law, that many other nations have yet to establish fully.

Those of us who live in the United States are fortunate to live in a democratic, open society. Gerald Gaus, a philosophy professor and the author of *The Tyranny of the Ideal: Justice in a Diverse Society*, underlines just how remarkable this is:

> The democratic open society isn't a dispiriting imperfect compromise between justice and the immorality and stupidity of most others. It's a moral achievement of the first order—perhaps one of the greatest moral achievements in human history. It allows an incredible array of diverse views to disagree, cooperate and learn from each other. . . . Once we appreciate that the open society is an achievement, we come to a deeper appreciation that moral improvement and change is not part of a philosophical campaign to secure utopia, but an endless, ongoing activity to alleviate the injustices that we now appreciate and which now confront us. We seldom agree about perfect justice, but we often concur about glaring injustices—they really do glare at us. And not only do we typically agree about these injustices, but it is much more likely that we have the social technology to ameliorate them. Again, we come back to [Karl] Popper. Grand schemes of reconstruction are practically certain to fail and too often bring disaster, while piecemeal social reform has very often succeeded.[18]

Gaus lays down the challenge that incrementalism takes up. For us, incrementalism is nothing less than the endless, ongoing effort to alleviate injustices. It is a mindset. It is a way of greeting the world in a spirit of optimism even in the face of the daily conflicts, disappointments, and tragedies that life throws at all of us. And it is our best hope for continuing to improve the world even in an age of radical rhetoric.

Acknowledgments

The story of this book begins, as all too many stories do these days, on the internet and, specifically, on Twitter.

In late 2020, Greg published an op-ed in *The Hill* entitled "In Defense of Incrementalism." The op-ed grew out of conversations that the two of us had been having as we attempted to make sense of a world that seemed to be spinning even faster than usual. Among other things, we were in the midst of a global pandemic and a high-stakes presidential election. A not-insignificant group of Americans professed belief in a theory advanced by QAnon that the government was controlled by Satan-worshipping pedophiles. Meanwhile, the streets were full of people protesting against police brutality and racial inequality. In some places, the discontent boiled over into rioting and looting. The homicide rate was shooting back up in New York and other cities. As a country, we seemed to have been transplanted back to the tumultuous days of 1968.

As in 1968, along with all of the unrest came calls for radical change. Those who supported Bernie Sanders's presidential campaign proclaimed their desire to remake our country. The Black Lives Matter protests quickly morphed into calls to defund the police and abolish prisons. And Donald Trump, chaos agent extraordinaire, loomed over it all, threatening the end of elitism (if you were a supporter) or the end of democracy (if you were not).

In the midst of the lockdown of 2020, the two of us spent many hours discussing all of these developments by phone, text, and email. We came to the conclusion that some of the lessons that we had learned over the years from our work attempting to reform the

criminal justice system—particularly about how hard it is to accomplish anything and how small changes can add up to something
significant over time—were not part of the public discourse. So we
decided to try to articulate these ideas. The result was the op-ed in
The Hill.

What happened next will not surprise anyone who has tried to advance a heterodox opinion on the internet. The op-ed didn't exactly
go viral, but it did engender a fair amount of reaction on Twitter, almost all of it negative. "When has incrementalism actually worked?
I'm sincerely asking," asked one commentator. Another wrote, "Finally
a clarion call for the same shit that's been suffocating everyone for the
last 60 years or so. Brave." (We're pretty sure that this was meant sar-
castically.) A third summed up the feelings of many readers by writing
simply, "Your opinion sucks."

At the same time, we shared the essay with a few dozen friends
via email. The reaction was very different. Not only did we get a lot
of positive feedback, but many people wrote back saying that, while
they agreed wholeheartedly with the ideas expressed in the essay, they
were reluctant to say so in public.

This combination—vitriol on the internet but endorsement
offline—suggested that the idea of incremental change had struck a
nerve. So we decided to write this book.

Turning an idea into a book is inevitably a team sport. We would
like to thank the following teammates, coaches, and trainers:

At Oxford University Press, Niko Pfund and David McBride
helped us sharpen our writing and structure our ideas.

John Bostwick helped tighten the Introduction.

Jeff Plaut and Will Jordan at Global Strategy Group helped us
think through our chapter on what the public wants. Thanks also to
Mark White at YouGov for his help with our polling on incremental
change.

Michael Ryan has been a generous champion of our work, including reviewing our manuscript and providing feedback.

Dave Metz offered us insightful feedback on several chapters.

We are flattered that Malcolm Feeley read the entire manuscript and made numerous suggestions for how we might improve it.

David Mayhew, Frances E. Lee, and James Curry spoke to us about their work and helped inform Chapter 1.

Joseph Durlak reviewed Chapter 2 and helped us get a better understanding of implementation science.

Ed Berkowitz reviewed Chapter 4 and provided important perspective on the development of New Deal–era social programs.

Neeraj Kaushal helped inform Chapter 6, including sharing her thoughts and written work on the hidden strengths of the immigration system.

Randall Woods reviewed Chapter 7 and provided important perspective on the Great Society.

Michael Hayes reviewed the Conclusion and offered us access to some of his unpublished writings.

Greg Weiner helped to teach us that almost everything we've thought about had already been said by Daniel Patrick Moynihan.

Special thanks to the New York City Criminal Justice Agency and the Center for Court Innovation for providing us with inspiration, an institutional base, and real-life examples of the benefits of incremental change.

Speaking of inspiration, in writing this book, we drew encouragement from a broad range of thinkers who have offered a vigorous defense of liberalism and democracy in recent books and essays. These include: Jonathan Chait, Tyler Cowen, Meghan Daum, Freddie deBoer, William Deresiewicz, Matt Feeney, Kmele Foster, Conor Friedersdorf, Francis Fukuyama, Nick Gillespie, Adam Gopnik, Martin Gurri, Jonathan Haidt, Katie Herzog, Randall Kennedy, Jay Caspian King, Yuval Levin, Mark Lilla, Michael Lind, Glenn Loury, John McWhorter, Louis Menand, Yascha Mounk, George Packer, Michael Powell, Jonathan Rauch, Russ Roberts, Kat Rosenfeld, George Saunders, Jesse Singal, Ethan Strauss, Ruy Teixeira, Batya Ungar-Sargon, Bari Weiss, Thomas Chatterton Williams, Wesley Yang, and Matt Yglesias.

Finally, we would like to offer the following personal thanks:

Greg:

To John Bostwick and Bill McConagha: thank you for your friend-ship over the past 40+ years and for helping me think through many of the issues in this book.

To John Feinblatt: thanks for giving me my big professional break and setting the professional bar for me.

To Dan Wilhelm, Tom Allon, Liz Glazer, and Courtney Bryan: thank you for helping to ease my transition to life after the Center for Court Innovation.

To Allan and Michele Berman: thanks for the faith you have always showed in me.

To M. J. Berman: thank you for being a great brother.

To Hannah and Milly Berman: thank you for the joy you have brought to my life and for your creativity, which has spurred me to try to follow in your footsteps.

To Carolyn Vellenga Berman: thanks for making me a better person. You are the best.

Aubrey:

To my colleagues at the New York City Criminal Justice Agency for tolerating my preoccupation with an "un-vision" for the agency and for proving, once and for all, that incremental change need not be slow or modest.

To Marie VanNostrand for our shared love of incremental change.

To my RRGFFL pals for keeping me sane, including my podcast co-host Dave Metz and frequent interlocutor Matt Josephs.

To Bob Fox, Anita Sperling, and Chris Fox for encouraging me to become a reader at a young age and for our shared interest in ideas and travel.

To Luna and Hazel Fox for your generous spirits, love of life, and Mario Party skills. I love you very much.

To mi milagro Robin Berg, for the wonderful life we have made together and our shared connections to friends and family.

Notes

INTRODUCTION

1. Ron Chernow, *Alexander Hamilton* (New York: Penguin Books, 2005), 246–48.
2. We are indebted to Yuval Levin for making this point.
3. Alexander Hamilton, *The Federalist Papers* (New York: Penguin Books, 2012), 1–6.
4. Ibram X. Kendi, "Patience Is a Dirty Word," *The Atlantic*, July 23, 2020, https://www.theatlantic.com/ideas/archive/2020/07/john-lewis-and-danger-gradualism/614512/.
5. Bruce Abramson, "The Conservative Temperament Is Dooming America," *RealClear Politics*, September 16, 2021, https://www.realclearpolitics.com/articles/2021/09/16/the_conservative_temperament_is_dooming_america_146415.html.
6. To those who will accuse us of "both-sidism": we do believe that both the left and the right are to blame for our current predicament. But that does not mean that both sides are *equally* responsible. Republicans, under the influence of Donald Trump, have clearly gone further to the extreme than Democrats, for example.
7. Eric Foner, "American Radicals and the Change We Could Believe In," *The Nation*, December 14, 2016, https://www.thenation.com/article/archive/teaching-the-history-of-radicalism-in-the-age-of-obama/.
8. Matthew Yglesias, "The Case against Crisis-Mongering," *Slow Boring*, August 12, 2021, https://www.slowboring.com/p/fake-crisis.
9. Martin Gurri, *The Revolt of the Public* (San Francisco: Stripe Press, 2018), 22.
10. Daniel Herriges, "Incremental Doesn't Mean Slow," *Strong Towns*, September 28, 2020, https://www.strongtowns.org/journal/2020/9/28/incremental-doesnt-mean-slow.

11. Quoted in Joshua L. Cherniss, *Liberalism in Dark Times: The Liberal Ethos in the Twentieth Century* (Princeton, NJ: Princeton University Press, 2021), 118.

12. It is worth noting that Congress has also come together to pass major, bipartisan legislation in moments of national crisis, such as the Covid-19 pandemic and the 2008 financial crisis.

13. Matt Ridley, "Why Is It Cool to Be Gloomy?," *Human Progress*, December 7, 2018, https://www.humanprogress.org/why-is-it-so-cool-to-be-gloomy/.

CHAPTER 1

1. Ezra Klein, "The Political Scientist Donald Trump Should Read," *Vox*, January 24, 2019, https://www.vox.com/policy-and-politics/2019/1/24/18193523/donald-trump-wall-shutdown-congress-polarization-frances-lee.

2. James R. Carroll, "Mitch McConnell under Fire for Saying Top Priority Is Making Obama One-Term President," *Louisville Courier-Journal*, October 26, 2010.

3. "Frances Lee on Why Bipartisanship Is Irrational," *Vox conversations*, accessed October 28, 2021, https://podcasts.apple.com/us/podcast/frances-lee-on-why-bipartisanship-is-irrational/id1081584611?i=1000428111876.

4. Sheryl Gay Stolberg and Nicholas Fandos, "As Gridlock Deepens in Congress, Only Gloom Is Bipartisan," *New York Times*, January 27, 2018, http://www.nytimes.com/2018/01/27/us/politics/congress-dysfunction-conspiracies-trump.html.

5. Aaron Blake, "Gridlock in Congress? It's Probably Even Worse Than You Think," *Washington Post*, May 29, 2014, https://www.washingtonpost.com/news/the-fix/wp/2014/05/29/gridlock-in-congress-its-probably-even-worse-than-you-think/.

6. Lee Drutman, "We Need Political Parties. But Their Rabid Partisanship Could Destroy American Democracy," *Vox*, September 5, 2017, https://www.vox.com/the-big-idea/2017/9/5/16227700/hyperpartisanship-identity-american-democracy-problems-solutions-doom-loop/.

7. Lawrence S. Rothenberg, *Policy Success in an Age of Gridlock* (Cambridge: Cambridge University Press, 2018), 75.

8. Nicholas Fandos, "House Backs Jan. 6 Commission, but Senate Path Dims," *New York Times*, May 19, 2021, https://www.nytimes.com/2021/05/19/us/politics/house-jan-6-commission.html.

9. Hailey Fuchs, "Senators Introduce Bipartisan Bill to Overhaul Postal Service," *New York Times*, May 19, 2021, https://www.nytimes.com/2021/05/19/us/politics/postal-service-reform-legislation.html.

10. James M. Curry and Frances E. Lee, *The Limits of Party: Congress and Lawmaking in a Polarized Era* (Chicago: University of Chicago Press, 2020), 17.

11. Interview with Frances E. Lee and James M. Curry, July 9, 2021.

12. This story is well documented in Ezra Klein, *Why We're Polarized* (New York: Simon & Schuster, 2020).

13. David R. Mayhew, *The Imprint of Congress* (New Haven, CT: Yale University Press, 2017), 3.

14. Interview with Lee and Curry.

15. Greg Iacurci, "States Will Start Cutting Off Federal Unemployment Benefits Soon. Here's a Map of Where (and How Soon) Aid Is Ending," *CNBC*, June 7, 2021, https://www.cnbc.com/2021/06/07/states-will-be-ending-federal-unemployment-benefits-this-week.html.

16. Mayhew, *The Imprint of Congress*, 107–13.

17. Greg Weiner, *Madison's Metronome: The Constitution, Majority Rule, and the Tempo of American Politics* (Lawrence: University Press of Kansas, 2012), 58–60.

18. Quoted in Jeanne Nienaber Clarke and Helen M. Ingram, "A Founder: Aaron Wildavsky and the Study of Public Policy," *Policy Studies Journal* (September 2010), https://www.researchgate.net/publication/229650696_A_Founder_Aaron_Wildavsky_and_the_Study_of_Public_Policy.

19. Aaron Wildavsky, *The Politics of the Budgetary Process* (Boston: Little, Brown, 1984), 13.

20. Ibid., 129.

21. Ibid., 136.

22. Ibid., 178.

23. Ibid., 149.

24. Albert O. Hirschman, *Shifting Involvements: Private Interests and Public Action* (Princeton, NJ: Princeton University Press, 2002), 95.

25. Charles Lindblom, "The Science of Muddling Through," *Public Administration Review* 19, no. 2 (Spring 1959): 86, https://faculty.washington.edu/mccurdy/SciencePolicy/Lindblom%20Muddling%20Through.pdf.

26. Rothenberg, Policy *Success in an Age of Gridlock.*

27. Coral Davenport and Lisa Friedman, "The Battle Lines Are Forming in Biden's Climate Push," *New York Times*, January 26, 2021, https://www.nytimes.com/2021/01/26/climate/biden-climate-change.html.

28. Michael Oakeshott, *Rationalism in Politics and Other Essays* (Indianapolis: Liberty Fund, 1991), 27.

29. David A. Good, "Still Budgeting by Muddling Through: Why Disjointed Incrementalism Lasts," *Policy and Society* 30 (2011): 42.

30. Alan Taylor, *Thomas Jefferson's Education* (New York: W. W. Norton, 2019), 213.

31. Charles Lindblom, "Still Muddling, Not Yet Through," *Public Administration Review* 39, no. 6 (November–December 1979): 520.

32. Martha Derthick, *Policymaking for Social Security* (Washington, DC: Brookings Institution, 1979), 367.

33. M. A. H. Dempster and Aaron Wildavsky, "On Change: Or, There Is No Magic Size for an Increment," *Political Studies* 27, no. 3 (December 1979): 371–89.

34. Chuck Klosterman, *The Nineties* (New York: Penguin Press, 2022), 158.

CHAPTER 2

1. Chris Cillizza, "13 Times That People Who Worked for Donald Trump Directly Disobeyed Him," *CNN Politics*, April 22, 2019, https://www.cnn.com/2019/04/22/politics/donald-trump-disobey-mueller-report/index.html.

2. Brendan Morrow, "Former Secretary of State Rex Tillerson Says He Often Had to Prevent Trump from Violating the Law," *The Week,* December 12, 2018, https://theweek.com/speedreads/811414/former-secretary-state-rex-tillerson-says-often-prevent-trump-from-violating-law.

3. Cillizza, https://www.cnn.com/2019/04/22/politics/donald-trump-disobey-mueller-report/index.html.

4. Mathew Daly, "Zinke: One-Third of Interior Employees Not Loyal to Trump," *Associated Press,* September 25, 2017, https://apnews.com/article/570c910d21be41869f76d45a2c55c359.

5. Maria Stephan, "Staying True to Yourself in the Age of Trump: A How-To Guide for Federal Employees," *Washington Post*, February 10, 2017, https://www.washingtonpost.com/news/democracy-post/wp/2017/02/10/staying-true-to-yourself-in-the-age-of-trump-a-how-to-guide-for-federal-employees/.

6. Laura Rosenberg, "Career Officials: You Are the Last Line of Defense against Trump," *Foreign Policy*, January 30, 2017, http://foreignpolicy.com/2017/01/30/career-officials-you-are-the-last-line-of-defense-against-trump/.

7. Sean Illing, "The 'Deep State' Is Real. But It's Not What Trump Thinks It Is," *Vox*, May 13, 2020, https://www.vox.com/policy-and-politics/2020/5/13/21219164/trump-deep-state-fbi-cia-david-rohde.

8. Michael Lipsky, *Street-Level Bureaucracy: Dilemmas of the Individual in Public Services* (New York: Russell Sage Foundation, 1980), 3.

9. Quoted in John DiIulio Jr., "What Happens in Real Bureaucracies," *The Regulatory Review*, July 10, 2012, https://www.theregreview.org/2012/07/10/diiulio-wilson-real-bureaucracy/.

10. Jeremy B. White, "California Prosecutors Revolt against DA's Social Justice Changes," *Politico*, January 25, 2021, https://www.politico.com/news/2021/01/25/george-gascon-california-social-justice-461667.

11. Joseph Durlak, Speech to the National Academies of Science, September 15, 2016. Available at: https://vimeo.com/182866175.

12. Joseph Durlak, "The Importance of Quality Implementation for Research, Practice, and Policy," *US Department of Health and Human Services*, January 31, 2013, https://aspe.hhs.gov/reports/importance-quality-implementation-research-practice-policy-0.

13. Lisbeth B. Schorr and Frank Farrow, "Expanding the Evidence Universe," *Center for the Study of Social Policy*, December 2011, https://cssp.org/wp-content/uploads/2019/04/Expanding-Evidence-the-Evidence-Universe_Doing-Better-by-Knowing-More_December-2011.pdf.

14. Randomized controlled trials, the so-called gold standard of social science research, are often fetishized to the exclusion of other kinds of evidence. Unless a program has a randomized controlled trial to document its effectiveness, it has often been difficult to generate the political will or the funding necessary to scale it up. Another problem is that these trials are best performed on a fairly narrow range of programs that target discrete problems and easily discernable populations. Complicated initiatives, with lots of moving parts that attempt to address multifaceted problems simultaneously, are much harder to measure.

15. In recent years, many foundations, nonprofits, and government agencies have started to incorporate the voices of those with "lived experience" into program design, leadership, and evaluation. This typically means a greater focus on involving the end users of social services and government systems—for example, formerly incarcerated individuals, survivors of domestic abuse, foster care graduates. While this movement has its excesses, it has made a valuable contribution to the field of social policy. There is, however, little evidence that policymakers are making an effort to engage frontline government workers in a similar fashion.

16. Kristin A. Moore et al., "Program Implementation: What Do We Know?," *Atlantic Philanthropies*, October 2006, https://www.childtrends.org/wp-content/uploads/2014/02/2006-41ProgramImplementation.pdf.

17. James Q. Wilson, *Bureaucracy* (New York: Basic Books, 2000), 344.

18. Matthew Yglesias, "DC's Teacher Compensation Reform Is Working," *Slow Boring*, August 26, 2021, https://www.slowboring.com/p/dcs-teacher-compensation-reform-is.

19. Quoted in Bernardo Zacko, "What I Learned When I Became a Bureaucrat," *Salon*, October 8, 2017, https://www.salon.com/2017/10/08/what-i-learned-when-i-became-a-bureaucrat/.

20. Charles R. Morris, *The Cost of Good Intentions: New York City and the Liberal Experiment* (New York: W. W. Norton, 1980), 204–5.

21. Dale Russakoff, *The Prize: Who's in Charge of America's Schools* (Boston: Houghton Mifflin Harcourt, 2015), 210.

22. Bob Hudson, David Hunter, and Stephan Peckham, "Policy Failure and the Policy-Implementation Gap: Can Policy Support Programs Help?," *Policy Design and Practice* 2, no. 1 (February 2019), https://www.tandfonline.com/doi/full/10.1080/25741292.2018.1540378.

CHAPTER 3

1. The tweet that got Lee Fang in trouble can be found here: https://twitter.com/lhfang/status/1268390704645943297.

2. Matt Taibbi, "The American Press Is Destroying Itself," *TK News*, June 12, 2020, https://taibbi.substack.com/p/the-news-media-is-destroying-itself.

3. Jonathan Chait, "The Still-Vital Case for Liberalism in a Radical Age," *New York*, June 11, 2020, https://nymag.com/intelligencer/amp/2020/06/case-for-liberalism-tom-cotton-new-york-times-james-bennet.html.

4. Fang's apology can be found here: https://s3.documentcloud.org/documents/6938336/Statement.pdf.

5. Jeffrey M. Jones, "Trump Third Year Sets New Standard for Party Polarization," *Gallup*, January 21, 2020, https://news.gallup.com/poll/283910/trump-third-year-sets-new-standard-party-polarization.aspx.

6. Amanda Ripley, "Toxic Conflict: How to Break the Spell," *Conflict*, February 1, 2021, https://www.amandaripley.com/blog/toxic-conflict-how-to-break-the-spell.

7. "The Partisan Divide on Political Values Grows Even Wider," *Pew Research Center*, October 5, 2017, https://www.pewresearch.org/politics/

2017/10/05/the-partisan-divide-on-political-values-grows-even-wider/.

8. "Political Polarization in the American Public," *Pew Research Center*, June 12, 2014, https://www.pewresearch.org/politics/2014/06/12/political-polarization-in-the-american-public/.

9. Eitan Hersh, "College-Educated Voters Are Ruining American Politics," *The Atlantic*, January 20, 2020, https://www.theatlantic.com/ideas/archive/2020/01/political-hobbyists-are-ruining-politics/605212/.

10. Interview with Greg Berman, August 15, 2021.

11. Mark Blumenthal, "In 2021 Even the Weather Is Politicized," *YouGov America*, August 17, 2021, https://today.yougov.com/topics/politics/articles-reports/2021/08/17/2021-even-weather-politicized.

12. Adam D. I. Kramer, Jamie E. Guillory, and Jeffrey T. Hancock, "Experimental Evidence of Massive-Scale Emotional Contagion through Social Networks," *Proceedings of the National Academy of Sciences*, June 2014, https://www.pnas.org/content/111/24/8788.

13. "'Likes' and 'Shares' Teach People to Express More Outrage Online," *EurekAlert,* August 13, 2021, https://www.eurekalert.org/news-releases/924791.

14. Wesley Yang's tweet can be found here: https://twitter.com/wesyang/status/1052945621932363776.

15. Dan Yankelovich and Will Friedman, *Toward Wiser Public Judgment* (Nashville: Vanderbilt University Press, 2011), 28.

16. Christopher Lasch, *The Revolt of the Elites and the Betrayal of Democracy* (New York: W. W. Norton, 1995), 20.

17. Ibid., 27.

18. The majority of Americans do not use Twitter. Nonetheless, the platform is enormously influential due to its popularity among the "thinking classes." According to Jeff Plaut of the Global Strategy Group, "While Americans don't talk to each other on Twitter, reporters do. Hence its outsized influence."

19. Jeffrey M. Jones and Lydia Saad, "U.S. Support for More Government Inches Up, but Not for Socialism," *Gallup*, November 18, 2019, https://news.gallup.com/poll/268295/support-government-inches-not-socialism.aspx.

20. "Taxes," *Gallup*, accessed October 14, 2021, https://news.gallup.com/poll/1714/taxes.aspx.

21. Frank Newport, "Public Opinion, the Role of Government, and the Candidates," *Gallup*, November 27, 2019, https://news.gallup.com/opin

ion/polling-matters/268799/public-opinion-role-government-can
didates.aspx.

22. Matt Grossman, "Voters Like a Political Party until It Passes Laws,"
FiveThirtyEight, October 4, 2018, https://fivethirtyeight.com/features/
voters-like-a-political-party-until-it-passes-laws/.

23. Justin Fox, "Americans Sure Do Agree on a Lot," *Bloomberg*, December
14, 2020, https://www.bloomberg.com/opinion/articles/2020-12-14/
polling-shows-americans-agree-on-trade-immigration-climate.

24. Will Friedman and David Schleifer, "Hidden Common Ground: Why
Americans Aren't as Divided on Issues as We Appear to Be," *USA Today*,
April 27, 2021, https://www.usatoday.com/story/opinion/2021/04/
27/case-unity-americans-arent-divided-issues-appears-column/719
0411002/.

25. "Reimagining Rights and Responsibilities in the United States,"
Harvard Kennedy School Carr Center for Human Rights Policy, accessed
October 14, 2021, https://carrcenter.hks.harvard.edu/reimagining-rig
hts-responsibilities-united-states.

26. Caitlin Oprysko, "Poll: Americans United on a Slew of Issues, despite
Contentious Election Season," *Politico*, September 15, 2020, https://
www.politico.com/news/2020/09/15/election-season-americans-uni
ted-issues-poll-414687.

27. Stephen Hawkins, Daniel Yudkin, Miriam Juan-Torres, and Tim
Dixon, "Hidden Tribes: A Study of America's Polarized Landscape,"
More in Common, 2018, https://hiddentribes.us/media/qfpekz4g/hidde
n_tribes_report.pdf.

28. Emily Cochrane, "Senate Democrats Begin $3.5 Trillion Push for 'Big,
Bold Social Change," *New York Times*, August 9, 2021, https://www.nyti
mes.com/2021/08/09/us/politics/senate-budget.html.

29. Paul Krugman, "How Change Happens," *New York Times*, January 22,
2016, https://www.nytimes.com/2016/01/22/opinion/how-change-
happens.html.

30. Lisa Lerer, "Obama Says Average American Doesn't Want to 'Tear
Down System," *New York Times*, November 15, 2019, https://www.nyti
mes.com/2019/11/15/us/politics/barack-obama-2020-dems.html.

31. David Shor's tweet can be found here: https://twitter.com/davidshor/
status/1296811217152102400?lang=en.

32. "Who's Afraid of a Big Bad Poll?," *The Weeds*, September 3, 2021, https://
podcasts.apple.com/us/podcast/whos-afraid-of-a-big-bad-poll/id104
2433083?i=1000534217576.

33. It is also worth noting that we conducted this survey while the Democrats controlled the White House, which likely had a dampening effect on Republican interest in bold change (and vice versa for Democrats).

34. Hannah Gilberstadt and Andrew Daniller, "Liberals Make Up the Largest Share of Democratic Voters, but Their Growth Has Slowed in Recent Years," *Pew Research Center*, January 17, 2020, https://www.pewresearch.org/fact-tank/2020/01/17/liberals-make-up-largest-share-of-democratic-voters/.

35. "Differences in How Democrats and Republicans Behave on Twitter," *Pew Research Center*, October 15, 2020, https://www.pewresearch.org/politics/2020/10/15/differences-in-how-democrats-and-republicans-behave-on-twitter/.

36. "Communicating about Crisis," *Global Strategy Group*, July 7, 2021, https://navigatorresearch.org/wp-content/uploads/2021/07/Navigator-Update-07.07.21.pdf.

37. Lydia Saad, "Black Americans Want Police to Retain Local Presence," *Gallup*, August 5, 2020, https://news.gallup.com/poll/316571/black-americans-police-retain-local-presence.aspx.

38. Ibid.

39. Susan Page and Ella Lee, "Exclusive: In Poll, Only 1 in 5 Say Police Treat People Equally Even as Worries about Crime Surge," *USA Today*, July 8, 2021, https://www.usatoday.com/story/news/politics/2021/07/08/poll-worries-crime-most-say-police-dont-treat-all-equally/7880911002/.

40. Susan Page et al., "Exclusive Poll Finds Detroit Far More Worried about Public Safety Than Police Reform," *USA Today*, July 25, 2021, https://www.usatoday.com/story/news/politics/2021/07/25/detroit-police-reform-public-safety-defund-suffolk-poll/8001468002/.

41. Steve Crabtree, "Most Americans Say Policing Needs 'Major Changes,'" *Gallup*, July 22, 2020, https://news.gallup.com/poll/315962/americans-say-policing-needs-major-changes.aspx.

42. "America's Hidden Common Ground on Racism and Police Reform," *Public Agenda*, June 29, 2020, https://www.publicagenda.org/reports/americas-hidden-common-ground-on-police-reform-and-racism-in-america/.

43. Fox, "Americans Sure Do Agree on a Lot."

44. Will Friedman, "The Problem of Public Judgment in a Digital and Divisive Age," *Public Agenda*, September 2019, https://www.publi

cagenda.org/wp-content/uploads/2019/10/PA-Paper-DigitalAge-v5_FINAL.pdf.

CHAPTER 4

1. John R. Commons, "Karl Marx and Samuel Gompers," *Political Science Quarterly* 41, no. 2 (1926): 284.
2. By contrast, the Works Progress Administration, launched in 1935, put 8.5 million people to work (and absorbed 7.5 percent of the US GDP) before it was dissolved in 1943. The National Recovery Administration, which was established in 1933 to strengthen central government control over broad swaths of private industry, was unanimously declared unconstitutional by the US Supreme Court in 1935, though parts of the NRA lived on in other forms.
3. Theron F. Schlabach, *Edwin E. Witte: Cautious Reformer* (Madison: State Historical Society of Wisconsin, 1969), 77.
4. Edwin Amenta, *When Movements Matter: The Townsend Plan & The Rise of Social Security* (Princeton, NJ: Princeton University Press, 2006), 35.
5. Martha Derthick, *Policymaking for Social Security* (Washington, DC: Brookings Institution, 1979), 193.
6. Amenta, *When Movements Matter*, 1.
7. Derthick, *Policymaking for Social Security*, 194.
8. Amenta, *When Movements Matter*, 194.
9. Schlabach, *Edwin E. Witte*, 111.
10. As a sign of how important FDR thought this message was, he repeated it verbatim in his remarks attached to the 1939 Social Security Act Amendments.
11. Noncitizens can also get a Social Security number if they work for a US employer.
12. Arthur J. Altmeyer, *The Formative Years of Social Security: A Chronicle of Social Security Legislation and Administration, 1934–1954* (Madison: University of Wisconsin Press, 1968), 66–70.
13. Subsequent historical scholarship has cast doubt on the idea that the Supreme Court intentionally changed its ruling on Social Security in reaction to FDR's court-packing plan, as in deliberations before FDR's plan was announced, a key swing vote (Justice Owen Roberts) had already signaled his willingness to support FDR's New Deal programs. Nonetheless, the phrase "the switch in time that saved nine" has entered into the popular imagination, and some historians argue that FDR's pressure campaign did indeed influence the Court's thinking.

William E. Leuchtenberg, "When Franklin Roosevelt Clashed with the Supreme Court—and Lost," *Smithsonian Magazine*, May 2005, https://www.smithsonianmag.com/history/when-franklin-roosevelt-clashed-with-the-supreme-court-and-lost-78497994/.

14. "Policy Basics: Top Ten Facts about Social Security," *Center for Budget and Policy Priorities,* August 2020, https://www.cbpp.org/research/social-security/top-ten-facts-about-social-security.

15. Alex Tabarrok, "Is Social Security a Ponzi Scheme?," *Marginal Revolution*, September 10, 2011, https://marginalrevolution.com/marginalrevolution/2011/09/is-social-security-a-ponzi-scheme.html.

16. Martha Derthick, *Policymaking for Social Security*, 232.

17. Schlabach, *Edwin E. Witte*, 170.

18. Ibid., 172.

19. Derthick, *Policymaking for Social Security*, 232.

20. Ibid., 224.

21. "Policy Basics: Top Ten Facts about Social Security," *Center on Budget and Policy Priorities,* August 13, 2020, https://www.cbpp.org/research/social-security/top-ten-facts-about-social-security.

22. Some scholars have suggested that the fifteen-year delay in including farm and domestic workers as Social Security beneficiaries was driven by explicit racial exclusion. Martha Derthick and Gareth Davies argue that the delay was driven by the incremental nature of Social Security: administrators were concerned about the technical and actuarial burdens of including agricultural employees working for small, informal businesses and households, but they thought these groups could be added later on (as in fact they were). And as Derthick and Davies point out, huge swaths of the 1935 workforce were also originally excluded for non-racial reasons, including all government and nonprofit employees and medical professionals based on "familiar administrative difficulties, perceived actuarial obstacles, and the belief that many members of these groups would not desire to be included in this scheme of compulsory taxation." See Gareth Davis and Martha Derthick, "Race and Social Welfare Policy: The Social Security Act of 1935," *Political Science Quarterly* 112, no. 2 (Summer 1997): 226, https://doi.org/10.2307/2657939.

23. Derthick, *Policymaking for Social Security*, 274.

24. "Looking Backward," Wikipedia, accessed October 31, 2021, https://en.wikipedia.org/wiki/Looking_Backward.

25. Derthick, *Policymaking for Social Security*, 9.

26. Ibid., 291.

27. Jonathan Cohn, *The Ten Year War: Obamacare and the Unfinished Crusade for Universal Coverage* (New York: St. Martin's Press, 2021).

28. Derthick, *Policymaking for Social Security*, 17.

CHAPTER 5

1. "The 101 Best New York Movies of All Time," *Time Out New York*, April 6, 2019, https://www.timeout.com/newyork/film/best-new-york-movies.

2. Vincent Canby, "Escape from New York," *New York Times*, July 10, 1981, https://www.nytimes.com/1981/07/10/movies/escape-from-new-york.html.

3. Cosell's actual words can be heard here: https://www.youtube.com/watch?v=bnVH-BE9CU0.

4. Kevin Baker, "Welcome to Fear City," *The Guardian,* May 18, 2015, https://www.theguardian.com/cities/2015/may/18/welcome-to-fear-city-the-inside-story-of-new-yorks-civil-war-40-years-on.

5. Samuel M. Ehrenhalt, "Economic and Demographic Change: The Case of New York City," *Monthly Labor Review*, February 1993, https://www.bls.gov/opub/mlr/1993/02/art4full.pdf.

6. Thomas Dyja, *New York, New York, New York* (New York: Simon & Schuster, 2021), 154

7. "Demographic History of New York City," *Wikipedia*, accessed October 16, 2021, https://en.wikipedia.org/wiki/Demographic_history_of_New_York_City.

8. Malcolm Gladwell, *The Tipping Point* (Boston: Little, Brown, 2000), 137–38.

9. Kevin Drum, "Lead: America's Real Criminal Element," *Mother Jones*, January/February 2016, https://www.motherjones.com/environment/2016/02/lead-exposure-gasoline-crime-increase-children-health/.

10. "The New York 'Miracle,'" *The Crime Report*, October 17, 2011, https://thecrimereport.org/2011/10/17/2011-10-the-new-york-miracle/.

11. Dyja, *New York, New York, New York*, 265.

12. Chris Smith, "The Controversial Crime-Fighting Program That Changed Big-City Policing Forever," *New York,* accessed October 17, 2021, https://nymag.com/intelligencer/2018/03/the-crime-fighting-program-that-changed-new-york-forever.html.

13. Gladwell, *The Tipping Point*, 145.

14. Preeti Chauhan et al., "Trends in Misdemeanor Arrests in New York," *John Jay College of Criminal Justice,* October 28, 2014, "https://datacoll

aborativeforjustice.org/wp-content/uploads/2020/04/Misdemeanor-Report.pdf.

15. https://criminaljustice.cityofnewyork.us/individual_charts/misdemeanor-arrests/.

16. "Stop and Frisk Data," ACLU of New York, accessed October 17, 2021, https://www.nyclu.org/en/stop-and-frisk-data.

17. Patrick Sharkey, *Uneasy Peace: The Great Crime Decline, the Renewal of City Life, and the Next War on Violence* (New York: W. W. Norton, 2018), 53.

18. Vincent Schiraldi, "New York City Success Story: Leaving 'Mass Imprisonment' Behind," *The Crime Report*, February 20, 2020, https://thecrimereport.org/2020/02/20/new-york-city-success-story-leaving-mass-imprisonment-behind/.

19. "Trends in Crime and Justice," Presentation by Jeremy Travis at New York Law School, March 8, 2019.

20. Aubrey Fox and Stephen Koppel Jr., "Pretrial Release without Money: New York City, 1987–2018," *New York City Criminal Justice Agency*, March 2019, https://www.nycja.org/assets/CJA_RWM_March_2019.pdf.

21. Adam Gopnik, "The Caging of America," *New Yorker*, January 30, 2012.

22. Michael Rempel and Joanna Weill, "One Year Later: Bail Reform and Judicial Decision-Making in New York City," *Center for Court Innovation*, April 2021, https://www.courtinnovation.org/sites/default/files/media/document/2021/One_Year_Bail_Reform_NYS.pdf.

23. Rempel and Weill, "One Year Later."

24. Beth Fertig and Jake Dobkin, "City's Jail Population Rises after Bail Reform Gets a Rewrite," *The Gothamist*, December 21, 2020, https://gothamist.com/news/citys-jail-population-rises-after-bail-reform-gets-a-rewrite.

25. Ben Chapman, "New York City Police Solve Fewer Crimes in Pandemic," *Wall Street Journal*, December 2, 2020, https://www.wsj.com/articles/new-york-city-police-solve-fewer-crimes-in-pandemic-11606917600.

26. Stephen Lepore, "NYPD: Shootings Up 166%, Fueling NYC Crime Surge," *News 10*, May 19, 2021, https://www.news10.com/news/ny-news/nypd-shootings-up-166-fueling-nyc-crime-surge.

27. Bobby Cuza, "Exclusive Poll: Crime Takes Center Stage in Mayor's Race, Fueling Support for Eric Adams," *NY1*, June 7, 2021, https://www.ny1.com/nyc/all-boroughs/decision-2021/2021/06/07/crime-takes-center-stage-in-mayor-s-race--fueling-support-for-eric-adams.

28. Carl Campanile, "Former NYPD Boss Says Adams' Primary Win 'Good News' for NYC," *New York Post*, July 7, 2021, https://nypost.com/2021/07/07/bill-bratton-calls-adams-primary-win-good-news-for-nyc.

29. George Kelling, "How New York Became Safe: The Full Story," *City Journal*, 2009, https://www.city-journal.org/html/how-new-york-became-safe-full-story-13197.html.

CHAPTER 6

1. Sabrina Rodriquez, "Trump's Partially Built, 'Big Beautiful Wall,'" *Politico*, January 12, 2021, https://www.politico.com/news/2021/01/12/trump-border-wall-partially-built-458255.

2. "Afghanistan: How Many Refugees Are There and Where Will They Go?," *BBC News*, August 31, 2021, https://www.bbc.com/news/world-asia-58283177.

3. Michael D. Shear, "The Biden Administration Will Raise the Cap on Refugee Admissions to 125,000," September 20, 2021, *New York Times*, https://www.nytimes.com/2021/09/20/us/politics/biden-refugee-cap.html.

4. Andrew Sullivan, "How Biden Could Bring Back Trump," *Weekly Dish*, October 1, 2021, https://andrewsullivan.substack.com/p/how-biden-could-bring-back-trump.

5. Quinn Scanlan, "At Critical Moment, Confidence in Biden's Ability to Handle Range of Issues Eroding," *ABC News*, September 29, 2021, https://abcnews.go.com/Politics/critical-moment-confidence-bidens-ability-handle-range-issues/story?id=80290520&cid=social_fb_abcn.

6. Neeraj Kaushal, *Blaming Immigrants: Nationalism and the Economics of Global Movement* (New York: Columbia University Press, 2019), 64.

7. Abby Budiman, "Key Findings about U.S. Immigrants," *Pew Research Center*, August 20, 2020, https://www.pewresearch.org/fact-tank/2020/08/20/key-findings-about-u-s-immigrants/.

8. "International Students in USA (by the Facts & Figures)," *Admissionly*, https://admissionly.com/international-students-in-usa-statistics/.

9. Kaushal, *Blaming Immigrants*, 66.

10. Aubrey Fox interview with Neeraj Kaushal, September 29, 2021.

11. Francesco Castelli, "Drivers of Migration: Why Do People Move?," *Journal of Travel Medicine* 25, no. 1 (2018), https://academic.oup.com/jtm/article/25/1/tay040/5056445.

12. Orli Belman, "Immigration Boosts U.S. Life Expectancy, according to USC/Princeton Study," *USC Leonard David School of Gerontology*,

September 20, 2021, https://gero.usc.edu/2021/09/30/immigration-boosts-u-s-life-expectancy-according-to-usc-princeton-study/.

13. Arun S. Hendi and Jessica Y. Ho, "Immigration and Improvements in American Life Expectancy," *SSM—Population Health* 15 (September 2021), https://www.sciencedirect.com/science/article/pii/S235282732 1001890.

14. Paola Scommegna, "Which Country Has the Oldest Population? It Depends on How You Define 'Old,'" *PRB*, September 25, 2019, https://www.prb.org/resources/which-country-has-the-oldest-population/.

15. Martin Gelin, "Japan Radically Increased Immigration—And No One Protested," *Foreign Policy*, June 23, 2020, https://foreignpolicy.com/2020/06/23/japan-immigration-policy-xenophobia-migration/.

16. Eshe Nelson and Megan Specia, "Gas Shortages Awaken Britain to Some Crucial Workers: Truck Drivers," *New York Times,* September 29, 2021, https://www.nytimes.com/2021/09/29/business/gas-shortages-britain-truck-drivers.html.

17. "Understanding Canada's Immigration System," *Government of Canada*, https://www.canada.ca/en/immigration-refugees-citizenship/campaigns/irregular-border-crossings-asylum/understanding-the-system.html.

18. Kaushal, *Blaming Immigrants*, 71–73.

19. "How Foreign Workers in the USA Can Move to Canada," *Moving 2 Canada*, https://moving2canada.com/h1b-workers-moving-usa-to-canada/.

20. Jia Lynn Yang, *One Mighty and Irresistible Tide: The Epic Struggle over American Immigration, 1924–1965* (New York: W. W. Norton, 2020), 238.

21. Steven M. Gillon, "How a Little Known '60s Congressman Unwittingly Upended U.S. Immigration," *The History Channel*, February 2, 2018, https://www.history.com/news/1965-immigration-policy-lyndon-johnson.

22. Ibid.

23. Yang, *One Mighty and Irresistible Tide*, 264.

24. Quoctrung Bui and Cailin Dickerson, "What Can the U.S. Learn from How Other Countries Handle Immigration?," *New York Times*, February 16, 2018, https://www.nytimes.com/interactive/2018/02/16/upshot/comparing-immigration-policies-across-countries.html.

25. Ibid.

26. Jane Hong, "The Law That Created Illegal Immigration," *Los Angeles Times*, October 2, 2015, https://www.latimes.com/opinion/op-ed/la-oe-1002-hong-1965-immigration-act-20151002-story.html.

27. Douglas S. Massey, "Immigration Policy Mismatches and Counterproductive Outcomes: Unauthorized Migration to the U.S. in Two Eras," *Comparative Migration Studies,* June 25, 2020, https://comparativemigrationstudies.springeropen.com/articles/10.1186/s40878-020-00181-6.

28. Robert Pear, "President Signs Landmark Bill on Immigration," *New York Times,* November 7, 1986, https://www.nytimes.com/1986/11/07/us/president-signs-landmark-bill-on-immigration.html.

29. "E-Verify Brief History and Overview," *Bipartisan Policy Center,* April 2013, https://bipartisanpolicy.org/download/?file=/wp-content/uploads/2019/03/E-verify-background-web-10-2-2_format.pdf.

30. Alex Nowrasteh, "Why E-Verify Is failing," *Politico,* October 29, 2019, https://www.politico.com/news/agenda/2019/10/29/e-verify-immigration-060347.

31. Miriam Jordan, "Making President Trump's Bed: A Housekeeper without Papers," *New York Times,* December 6, 2018, https://www.nytimes.com/2018/12/06/us/trump-bedminster-golf-undocumented-workers.html.

32. "History of ICE," U.S. Immigration and Customs Enforcement, https://www.ice.gov/history.

33. "Trump Administration Continues to Expand Interior Immigration Enforcement," Cato at Liberty, https://www.cato.org/blog/trump-administration-continues-expand-interior-immigration-enforcement.

34. Aubrey Fox interview with Neeraj Kaushal, September 29, 2021.

35. Ben Gitis and Laura Collins, "The Budgetary and Economic Costs of Addressing Unauthorized Immigration: Alternative Strategies," *American Action Forum,* March 6, 2015, https://www.americanactionforum.org/research/the-budgetary-and-economic-costs-of-addressing-unauthorized-immigration-alt/.

36. "State Laws Related to Immigration and Immigrants," *National Conference for State Legislators,* March 8, 2021, https://www.ncsl.org/research/immigration/state-laws-related-to-immigration-and-immigrants.aspx.

37. Kaushal, *Blaming Immigrants,* 94.

38. "Economic Cost of Texas House Bill 413 and Senate Bill 576," New American Economy, https://www.immigrationresearch.org/system/files/TX_TuitionBrief.pdf.

39. Robert Suro, "Where to Go for Real Immigration Reform," *New York Times,* September 15, 2015, https://www.nytimes.com/2015/09/16/opinion/where-to-go-for-real-immigration-reform.html.

40. Kaushal, *Blaming Immigrants,* 77.

41. Luke Broadwater, "Democrats Dealt a Blow on Immigration Plans," *New York Times,* September 19, 2021, https://www.nytimes.com/2021/09/19/us/politics/immigration-citizenship.html.

42. Aubrey Fox interview with Neeraj Kaushal, September 29, 2021.

43. "Immigration's Effect on the Social Security System," *Bipartisan Research Center,* November 2018, https://bipartisanpolicy.org/download/?file=/wp-content/uploads/2019/03/Immigrations-Effect-on-the-Social-Security-System.pdf.

44. Zaid Jilani, "Immigrants Are Far More Patriotic Than the Right Fears or the Left Hopes," *Persuasion,* July 29, 2020, https://www.persuasion.community/p/immigrants-are-far-more-patriotic.

45. Jeffrey S. Passel and D'Vera Cohn, "Immigrant Total Dips to Lowest Level in a Decade," *Pew Research Center,* https://www.pewresearch.org/hispanic/wp-content/uploads/sites/5/2019/03/Pew-Research-Center_2018-11-27_U-S-Unauthorized-Immigrants-Total-Dips_Updated-2019-06-25.pdf.

46. Jeremy L. Neufeld, Lindsay Milliken, and Doug Rand, "Stop the Incinerator: The High Cost of Green Card Slots Going Unused and the Benefits of Recapturing Them," *Niskanen Center,* June 23, 2021, https://www.niskanencenter.org/stop-the-incinerator-the-high-cost-of-green-card-slots-going-unused-and-the-benefits-of-recapturing-them/.

CHAPTER 7

1. Karen Tumulty, "The Great Society at 50," *Washington Post,* May 17, 2014, https://www.washingtonpost.com/sf/national/2014/05/17/the-great-society-at-50/.

2. Robert Caro, *Master of the Senate* (New York: Vintage Press, 2003).

3. Melissa Block, "LBJ Carried Poor Texas Town with Him in Civil Rights Fight," *National Public Radio,* April 11, 2014, https://www.npr.org/2014/04/11/301820334/lbj-carried-cotulla-with-him-in-civil-rights-fight.

4. Quoted in Woods, 53–54.

5. Quoted in ibid., 54–57.

6. Joshua Zeitz, *Building the Great Society: Inside Lyndon Johnson's White House* (New York: Viking, 2018), 69.

7. Henry J. Aaron, *Politics and the Professors: The Great Society in Perspective* (Washington, DC: Brookings Institution, 1978), 8–9.

8. Daniel Patrick Moynihan, *Maximum Feasible Misunderstanding: Community Action in the War on Poverty* (New York: Free Press, 1970), 25.

9. Zeitz, *Building the Great Society*, 184–85.

10. Moynihan, *Maximum Feasible Misunderstanding*, liv.

11. Ibid., 51–59.

12. Aaron, *Politics and the Professors*, 30–31.

13. Woods, 200.

14. Bernard J. Frieden and Marshall Kaplan, *The Politics of Neglect: Urban Aid from Model Cities to Revenue Sharing* (Cambridge, MA: MIT Press, 1975), 30.

15. Amity Shlaes, *Great Society: A New History* (New York: HarperCollins, 2019), 40–41.

16. Ibid., 151–52.

17. Charles Morris, *A Time of Passion: America 1960–1980* (New York: Penguin Books, 1986), 93–94.

18. "9 in Youth Project Linked to Leftists," *New York Times*, August 19, 1964, https://www.nytimes.com/1964/08/19/archives/9-in-youth-project-linked-to-leftists.html.

19. "Mobilization for Youth Sets Up Structure with 2 Co-Directors," *New York Times*, September 15, 1964, https://www.nytimes.com/1964/09/15/archives/mobilization-for-youth-sets-up-structure-with-2-codirectors.html.

20. Woods, 201.

21. Ibid., 68.

22. Moynihan, *Maximum Feasible Misunderstanding*, 111.

23. Community Action and the Office of Economic Opportunity would later be abolished by President Richard Nixon, although some of the program's ideals lived on in VISTA, the domestic version of the Peace Corps—later absorbed by President Bill Clinton's AmeriCorps initiative. There are still hundreds of governmental and nonprofit agencies with "Community Action" in their title. Aubrey served as a VISTA volunteer for a Community Action Agency in San Antonio, Texas, in 1994; the language of "maximum feasible participation" was still very much in use at that time.

24. Shlaes, *Great Society*, 82–84.

25. Frieden and Kaplan, *The Politics of Neglect*, 42.

26. Woods, 256.

27. Frieden and Kaplan, *The Politics of Neglect*, 47–49.

28. Woods, 258.

29. Frieden and Kaplan, *The Politics of Neglect*, 74.

30. Ibid., 85.

31. Ibid., 236.

32. Ibid., 36.
33. Woods, 259.
34. Frieden and Kaplan, *The Politics of Neglect*, 237–38.
35. Joshua Zeitz, "What Everyone Gets Wrong about LBJ's Great Society," *Politico*, January 18, 2018, https://www.politico.com/magazine/story/2018/01/28/lbj-great-society-josh-zeitz-book-216538/.
36. Ibid.
37. Aaron, *Politics and the Professors*, 4.
38. Nathan Glazer, *The Limits of Social Policy* (Cambridge, MA: Harvard University Press, 1990), 2.
39. Aaron, *Politics and the Professors*, 74–76.
40. Leah Gordon, "The Coleman Report and Its Critics: The Contested Meanings of Educational Equality in the 1960s and 1970s," *Process: A Blog for American History*, March 22, 2017, http://www.processhistory.org/gordon-coleman-report/.
41. Ibid., 17.
42. Greg Weiner, *American Burke: The Uncommon Liberalism of Daniel Patrick Moynihan* (Lawrence: University Press of Kansas, 2015), 2.
43. Kelsey Piper, "Science Has Been in a 'Replication Crisis' for a Decade. Have We Learned Anything?" *Vox*, October 14, 2020, https://www.vox.com/future-perfect/21504366/science-replication-crisis-peer-review-statistics.
44. Moynihan, *Maximum Feasible Misunderstanding*, 135.
45. Ibid., 189.

CHAPTER 8

1. Kerry A. Dolan, "Big Bet Philanthropy: How More Givers Are Spending Big and Taking Risks to Solve Society's Problems," *Forbes*, November 30, 2016, https://www.forbes.com/sites/kerryadolan/2016/11/30/big-bet-philanthropy-solving-social-problems/?sh=3a61380d79c5.
2. Aaron Timms, "George Packer's Center Cannot Hold," *New Republic*, September 13, 2021, https://newrepublic.com/article/163514/george-packer-last-best-hope-review-muddled-liberalism.
3. Martin O'Neill, "Against Incrementalism," *Boston Review*, August 18, 2021, https://bostonreview.net/politics/martin-oneill-go-big-ed-miliband.
4. Andrew Gawthorpe, "The Democrats Priority in Power Must Be to Stop Minority Rule," *The Guardian*, January 27, 2021, https://www.theguardian.com/commentisfree/2021/jan/27/the-democrats-priority-in-power-must-be-to-stop-minority-rule.

5. "Editorial: Incrementalism Has Failed to Protect Americans from the Violence of Racism," *Denver Post*, June 5, 2020, https://www.denverpost.com/2020/06/05/editorial-incrementalism-failed-police-force-violence-racism-george-floyd/.

6. Peter H. Schuck, "Militant Moderation," *American Purpose*, March 16, 2022, https://www.americanpurpose.com/articles/militant-moderation/.

7. David Samuels, "The Authority Blob," *Tablet*, September 10, 2021, https://www.tabletmag.com/sections/arts-letters/articles/authority-blob-roundtable.

8. Robert Kagan, "Our Constitutional Crisis Is Already Here," *Washington Post*, September 23, 2021, https://www.washingtonpost.com/opinions/2021/09/23/robert-kagan-constitutional-crisis/.

9. Oliver Burkeman, *Four Thousand Weeks: Time Management for Mortals* (New York: Farrar, Straus & Giroux, 2021), 98.

10. "Thomas Sowell: There Are No Solutions, Only Trade-offs," *YouTube*, August 10, 2013, https://www.youtube.com/watch?v=3_EtIWmja-4.

11. John Lewis, "It's Time to Dial Down the Political Rhetoric," *The Hill*, January 12, 2011, https://thehill.com/blogs/congress-blog/politics/137423-its-time-to-dial-down-the-political-rhetoric-rep-john-lewis.

12. Paige Fernandez and Taylor Pendergrass, "10 Things to Know about Combatting Violence in America," *ACLU*, September 7, 2021, https://www.aclu.org/news/criminal-law-reform/10-things-to-know-about-combating-violence-in-america/.

13. Greg Berman and Aubrey Fox, "Embracing Failure: Lessons for Court Managers," accessed October 12, 2021, https://www.courtinnovation.org/sites/default/files/Embracing_failure.pdf.

14. Paul Gary Wyckoff, *Policy & Evidence in a Partisan Age: The Great Disconnect* (Washington DC: Urban Institute Press, 2009), 3–4.

15. Darren Walker, "In Defense of Nuance," *Ford Foundation,* September 19, 2019, https://www.fordfoundation.org/just-matters/just-matters/posts/in-defense-of-nuance/.

16. "No New Jails: Activists Protest at Ford Foundation," *ArtForum*, September 27, 2019, https://www.artforum.com/news/no-new-jails-activists-protest-at-ford-foundation-80907.

17. "No New Jails NYC Response to MoreJustNYC: Free Them All," *Medium*, October 7, 2019, https://medium.com/@nonewjails.ny/no-new-jails-nyc-response-to-morejustnyc-free-them-all-d2c12 9c9e229.

18. John Herman, "Does This Moment in History Call for More 'Nuance' or Less," *New York Times*, October 16, 2018, https://www.nytimes.com/2018/10/16/magazine/does-this-moment-in-history-call-for-more-nuance-or-less.html.

19. Katie Reilly, "Read Hillary Clinton's 'Basket of Deplorables' Remarks about Trump Supporters," *Time*, September 10, 2016, https://time.com/4486502/hillary-clinton-basket-of-deplorables-transcript/.

20. "George Will: Republican Officeholders 'Are Terrified' of Their Voters," *YouTube*, September 16, 2021, https://www.youtube.com/watch?v=1vofmvlyww8.

21. Alec Tyson, "Partisans Say Respect and Compromise Are Important in Politics—Particularly from Their Opponents," *Pew Research Center*, June 19, 2019, https://www.pewresearch.org/fact-tank/2019/06/19/partisans-say-respect-and-compromise-are-important-in-politics-particularly-from-their-opponents/.

22. Jeremy Adelman, *Worldly Philosopher: The Odyssey of Albert O. Hirschman* (Princeton, NJ: Princeton University Press, 2013), 116–17.

23. Malcolm Gladwell, "The Gift of Doubt," *New Yorker*, June 24, 2013, https://www.newyorker.com/magazine/2013/06/24/the-gift-of-doubt.

CONCLUSION

1. Paul Goldberger, "Robert Moses, Master Builder, Is Dead at 92," *New York Times,* July 30, 1981, https://www.nytimes.com/1981/07/30/obituaries/robert-moses-master-builder-is-dead-at-92.html.

2. Revisionist historians have looked at the battle between Moses and Jacobs as an important episode of "NIMBY" resistance to development. Some critics have also come to see Jacobs as an advocate for gentrification.

3. Jone Johnson Lewis, "Jane Jacobs: New Urbanist Who Transformed City Planning," *ThoughtCo.*, August 14, 2019, https://www.thoughtco.com/jane-jacobs-biography-4154171.

4. Yuval Levin, "The History of the Left-Right Divide: A Centuries-Old Argument Defines Our Politics, and Offers a Way Forward," *Salon*, November 24, 2013, https://www.salon.com/2013/11/24/the_history_of_the_left_right_divide_a_centuries_old_argument_defines_our_politics_and_offers_a_way_forward/.

5. Quoted in Greg Weiner, *American Burke: The Uncommon Liberalism of Daniel Patrick Moynihan* (Lawrence: University Press of Kansas, 2015), 129.

6. This description of Popper, and the quotes from Popper's work, are taken from William Gorton, "Karl Popper: Political Philosophy," *Internet Encyclopedia of Philosophy*, accessed October 22, 2021, https://iep.utm. edu/popp-pol/#SH2b.

7. Fabian Society website, accessed October 22, 2021, https://fabians. org.uk.

8. Robert Sullivan, "Fabianism," *Modernist Journals Project*, accessed October 22, 2021, https://modjourn.org/essay/fabianism/.

9. Christian Adam et al., "On Democratic Intelligence and Failure: The Vice and Virtue of Incrementalism under Political Fragmentation and Policy Accumulation," *Governance*, April 1, 2021, https://onlinelibrary. wiley.com/doi/full/10.1111/gove.12595.

10. Climate change may be a rare issue that demands non-incremental change. But even here, we would argue that the perfect shouldn't be the enemy of the good. Following the path of incrementalism would still mean taking immediate action to move away from the current status quo. Incrementalism would also help environmental advocates deal with an inconvenient truth: they have *not* succeeded in convincing millions of Americans of the urgency of their cause. Forcing structural changes to the American economy that do not have massive public support is a sure recipe for social unrest.

11. Thomas Sowell, *A Conflict of Visions: Ideological Origins of Political Struggles* (New York: Basic Books, 2007), 30.

12. Ibid., 25.

13. Peter Kelley, "A Conversation with Dan Chirot about His New Book 'You Say You Want a Revolution' Exploring Radical Idealism, *UW News*, April 20, 2020, https://www.washington.edu/news/2020/04/ 20/a-conversation-with-dan-chirot-about-his-new-book-you-say-you-want-a-revolution-exploring-radical-idealism/.

14. Michael T. Hayes, *The Limits of Policy Change* (Washington, DC: Georgetown University Press, 2001), 4.

15. "Moderation as a Political Strategy: What Are the Lessons from History?," *Niskanen Center*, April 17, 2019, https://www.niskanencen ter.org/moderation-as-a-political-strategy-what-are-the-lessons-from-history/.

16. David Roberts, "This Is an Emergency, Damn It," *Vox*, February 23, 2019, https://www.vox.com/energy-and-environment/2019/2/23/ 18228142/green-new-deal-critics.

17. Philip E. Converse, "The Nature of Belief Systems in Mass Publics,"
    Critical Review 18, no. 1–3 (1964): 1–74, https://www.tandfonline.com/
    doi/pdf/10.1080/08913810608443650.

18. Richard Marshall, "The Tyranny of the Ideal," *3–16*, accessed October 22,
    2021, https://www.3-16am.co.uk/articles/the-tyranny-of-the-ideal?c=end-
    times-archive.

Index

For the benefit of digital users, indexed terms that span two pages (e.g., 52–53) may, on occasion, appear on only one of those pages.